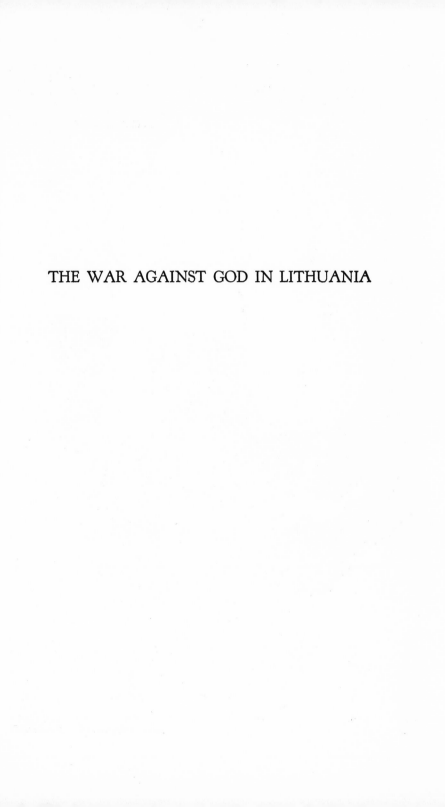

THE WAR AGAINST GOD IN LITHUANIA

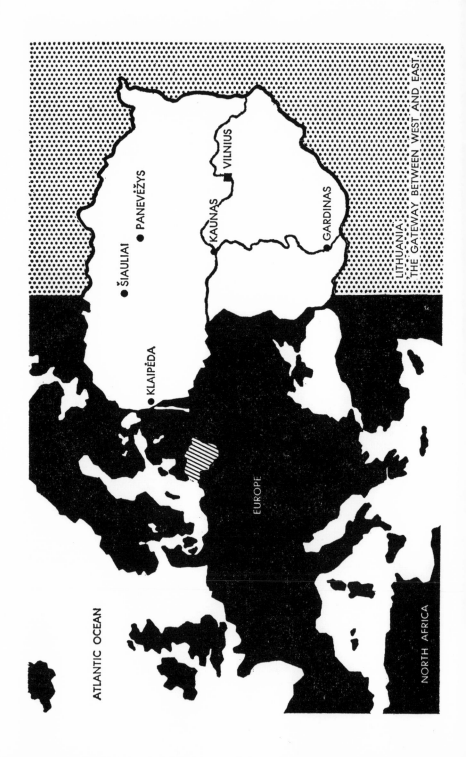

ATLANTIC OCEAN

KLAIPĖDA

ŠIAULIAI

PANEVĖŽYS

KAUNAS

VILNIUS

GARDINAS

EUROPE

NORTH AFRICA

LITHUANIA: THE GATEWAY BETWEEN WEST AND EAST.

THE WAR
AGAINST GOD
IN LITHUANIA

by
Dr. J. Savasis

Preface by
MOST REV. BISHOP EDWARD E. SWANSTROM

MANYLAND BOOKS, INC. • NEW YORK

THE WAR AGAINST GOD IN LITHUANIA

CONTENTS

PREFACE

THE WAR AGAINST GOD IN LITHUANIA presents a powerful factual evidence of the religious persecution practiced by the Communists today in that Soviet-occupied state. For more than five centuries, the predominantly Catholic Lithuanians have experienced every form of oppression and deprivation of religious freedom. Yet their nation has always survived, and they have become even more firm in their religious faith.

We know from history that other nations have suffered from similar persecutions. The Irish people, for example, were subjected to severe religious oppression. But they remained steadfast in their faith and most loyal to their clergy.

Materialistic communism cannot maintain domination over the faith of the human spirit. The totalitarian Soviet Russian regime must eventually collapse, and the Lithuanian nation, through its united efforts and prayers, will survive. *Christus vincit.*

I commend this book without reservation to the American reading public, for the information it provides about the religious persecution of the heroic Lithuanian people, and for the compelling arguments it offers for the need to use every available means to wipe out the Communist plague.

Auxiliary Bishop, Archdiocese of New York,
Executive Director, Catholic Relief Services—
National Catholic Welfare Conference

A NOTE ON LITHUANIA

LITHUANIANS lived on the Baltic shores long before the Christian era. At the beginning of the 15th century, Lithuania's frontiers extended from the Baltic to the Black Sea. Under the masterful leadership of Vytautas the Great, Grand Duke of Lithuania, the country was brought to a high rank among the European powers. Vytautas successfully defended Lithuania from the invasion of the Mongols and Tartars, who might otherwise have overrun all Europe.

Lithuania has long fought for its national existence. Down through the centuries, with Russia to the east, Germany to the west, and Poland to the southwest, Lithuania has had to protect itself continually from its neighbors, who were interested in claiming its fertile lands, enchanting forests and industrious inhabitants.

The growing threat of Moscow led to the establishment of the Polish-Lithuanian Commonwealth in 1569. In the 18th century, this Commonwealth was partitioned among Russia, Prussia, and Austria, with the greater part of Lithuania falling to tzarist Russia.

On February 16, 1918, Lithuania was able to regain its independence, and in 1921 it was admitted to membership in the League of Nations. During its 20 years of independence it made great strides in its political, economic, and cultural life.

Lithuanians are known for their rich folklore, beautiful songs, gay dances, and distinctive music and art. Their language, one of the most ancient languages of the world, is said to be closely related to Sanskrit. Lithuania's wayside shrines have always given expression to the deep faith of a God-loving people.

AREA: 25,167 square miles (65,200 square kilometers).

CLIMATE: The annual mean temperature is 43° F (6° C), or about that of Southern Sweden, or Northern Japan.

POPULATION: 2,917,000 in 1964 (3,215,000 in 1939). Demographers in the West calculate Lithuania's population losses from 1940 to 1959 as follows: (a) First Soviet occupation, 1940-41, 60♦,000; (b) German occupation, 1941-44, 250,000; (c) Second Soviet occupation, 1944-59, 570,000; (d) expatriates and refugees, 280,000.

CAPITAL: Vilnius, with a population of 264,000.

NATIONAL FLAG: Horizontal stripes of yellow, green and red.

STATE EMBLEM: Vytis—a mounted knight on a field of red.

NATIONAL HOLIDAY: February 16th—Day of the Restoration of Lithuania's Independence.

CHRONOLOGY

1251: Establishment of the Lithuanian Kingdom.

1569-1795: Lithuanian-Polish Commonwealth.

1795-1915: Lithuania under Russian rule.

1915-1918: Lithuania under German occupation.

1918: Restoration of Lithuania's Independence (Feb. 16).

1920: Peace Treaty with Soviet Russia (July 12).

1939: Secret Soviet-Nazi agreements against Lithuania (August 23 and September 28).

1940: Soviet invasion of Lithuania (June 15).

1940: Forcible incorporation of Lithuania into the USSR (August 3).

1941: Armed revolt against Soviet occupation and restoration of the Lithuanian Government (June 23).

1941-1944: Lithuania under German occupation.

1944: Second Soviet occupation of Lithuania.

1944-1952: Lithuanian guerilla warfare against the Soviets.

I. IN INDEPENDENT LITHUANIA

IN 1940, when the Soviet Russians occupied Lithuania, of the more than 3,000,000 inhabitants 85.5 per cent were Catholic. Among the remaining, 4.5 per cent were Protestant; 7.3 per cent, Jewish; and 2.5 per cent, Russian Orthodox. The fragmentary 0.2 per cent were divided among other faiths. Lithuanians comprised 80.6 per cent of the population; 94.4 per cent of them were Catholic.

In the two Catholic archdioceses and four dioceses there were 708 churches, 314 chapels, 73 monasteries, and 85 convents, with three archbishops, nine bishops, 1271 diocesan priests, and 580 monks, of whom 168 were priests. The four seminaries had an enrollment of 470. There were also 85 convents, with 950 nuns.

Nuns were in charge of 35 kindergartens, 10 orphanages and 25 homes for the aged. They also administered two hospitals, a youth center, and an institute for the deaf-and-dumb.

The armed forces, as well as prisons and hospitals, had chaplains. There were 18 Catholic primary schools and the same number of Catholic high schools. Religion was taught in all public schools. Atheists and irreligious people were practically non-existent.

In 1940 the outlawed Communist party had only 1741 members, of whom 616 were Lithuanian. Even after a year of pressure from the occupation forces, party membership totalled a mere 2504; of these, two-thirds were non-Lithuanian.

FREEDOM OF WORSHIP

The Constitution of independent Lithuania guaranteed full freedom of worship to all religious denominations. Relations between the Catholic Church and the state were defined by a Concordat with the Holy See in 1927. The clergy were exempted from military service and received a small salary from the state as partial compensation for church property seized by the czarist government. Some were also eligible for state pensions.

Religious activity flourished. It is estimated that about 800,000 belonged to various Catholic societies. The Catholic youth federation *Pavasaris* alone had 100,000 members. A children's organization, *Angelas Sargas,* numbered 60,-000; the Catholic Women's Society, 42,000; *Ateitininkai,* a federation of high school, college, and university students and graduates, 12,500; and Catholic Teachers, 1500.

The St. Casimir Society, founded in 1906 (two years after the Czar lifted the ban on the printing of Lithuanian books and newspapers in the Latin alphabet), had published 530 books in 2,294,000 copies by 1931. In the same period 5,000,000 copies of Catholic newspapers rolled off the presses of this single publishing society. In subsequent years of independence the number of Catholic publishers showed a marked increase. Their ranks included the Marian Fathers, the Jesuits, and the Franciscans, all making use of modern printing plants, book shops, and distribution agencies. Publications of the religious orders, wholly doctrinal, were widely read.

In 1935 there were 28 Lithuanian Catholic magazines and newspapers, which had a total circulation of 7,000,000. In addition to the weekly *Mūsų Laikraštis* (Our Newspaper) and the daily *XX Amžius* (The Twentieth Century), which ranked first in content and readership, numerous periodicals were designed for special interests, such as: *Logos,* for philosophy; *Soter,* theology; *Lietuvos Mokykla,* pedagogy; *Kosmos* and *Gamtos Draugas,* natural science; *Athenaeum,* history and history of literature; *Židinys, Naujoji Romuva* and others of general appeal. Every Catholic organization had its own publication.

A Department of Theology and Philosophy was a part of the University of Lithuania. The Catholics also had their own Academy of Arts and Sciences.

So extensive was Catholic influence in the country that in 1939 Pope Pius XII, accepting the credentials of Stasys Girdvainis, the new Lithuanian envoy to the Holy See, called Lithuania a frontline fortress of Catholic faith in northern Europe.

II. THE CHURCH UNDER THE COMMUNISTS

A CATHOLIC COUNTRY OCCUPIED

IN ACCORDANCE with a prearranged plan by Germany's Foreign Minister Ribbentrop and Soviet People's Commissar for Foreign Affairs Molotov for a Soviet takeover of the Baltic states, and in violation of the peace treaty of 1920 between Lithuania and the USSR, the non-aggression treaty of 1926 and the mutual assistance pact of 1939, on June 15, 1940, after a ten-hour ultimatum, thousands of Red Army troops, spearheaded by hundreds of Soviet tanks, marched into Lithuania. The Lithuanian government was removed and replaced by a provisional government selected by Moscow emissaries.

On July 14-15, parliamentary elections for a single list of Communist candidates were held. The turnout at the polls was exceedingly small (2,000 of the country's more influential citizenry were already under detention), but it was announced that 99.19 per cent of the voting population had cast their ballot. The newly-elected People's Diet convened on July 21 and, with the Red Army surrounding the assembly house, voted "unanimously" to nationalize all land-holdings, banks, and commercial and industrial firms, and declared Lithuania a Soviet Socialist Republic.

NATIONALIZATION AND CONFISCATION

Significantly, one of the first steps taken by the occupying powers, even before convening the so-called People's

Diet, was the June 25 announcement that the church was being separated from the state. Five days later, Archbishop Luigi Centoso, the Apostolic Nuncio from the Holy See, was ordered to leave the country.

When the land was nationalized, the former owners were permitted to retain up to 75 acres for their own use. Parishes, however, were left with a meager 7.5 acres, which included the ground occupied by the church and the parish cemetery. All compensation and pensions to the clergy were cut off, and the clergy's savings confiscated. Churches were deprived of all means of support. With the nationalization of business enterprises taking effect on August 6, Catholic printing plants and book stocks were confiscated, and all books of religious content were destroyed when they were found.

ATTACK ON RELIGION

On June 28, 1940, orders were issued forbidding the teaching of religion and the recitation of prayers in schools. Crucifixes and other religious objects were removed from the classrooms. The University's Department of Theology and Philosophy was abolished, and all private schools were nationalized. All chaplains were dismissed from their posts in the army, prisons, and hospitals. In place of religious instruction, lectures on Marxism and Leninism were introduced. When the priests persisted in holding classes in religion in their churches, sacristies, and private homes, some of them received the following document for their signature:

> I, the undersigned, a religious servant, residing at ———— village, ———— district and ———— county, testify by my signature, that on April ————, 1941, I received a formal announcement forbidding the giving of religious instruction to school children and those of

pre-school age, at school, at their homes or at my quarters—in a word, anywhere. Similarly, I have no right
to discuss religious questions with them. I also understand that, failing to observe this order, I shall be liable
to legal action.[1]

The Communists made every effort to induce the adult
population to "forget religion." They employed all possible
means to isolate the church from public life. When strong
anti-religious propaganda did not produce the desired effect,
the Communists took other measures. Government workers,
and especially teachers, were watched closely to prevent them
from attending church and from maintaining friendly relations with the clergy. Those caught going to church were
summoned before Communist authorities and threatened
with punishment.

In their assault on "superstitions of the masses," the
Communists abolished religious feast-days. Street processions
of the Feast of Corpus Christi were banned. Christmas and
Easter were declared work days; those who missed work or
school on those days were punished. Sundays, too, were often
made work days, especially when a Communist holiday
occurred in the same week.

PRESSURE ON PRIESTS

When the Communists took over the seminaries,[2] they
thought they had struck at the very root of the church's
existence. By confiscating the church property and leaving
the clergy without means of support and even without a
place to live, they hoped to end the clergy's influence over

---

[1] Jean Mauclère, La situation de l'Eglise Catholique en Lituanie, 1950,
Paris, 1950.

[2] Vilkaviškis and Telšiai seminaries were closed completely and only the
seminary at Kaunas was permitted operation on a very restricted scale.

the people. Now, with strongly waged propaganda, they would deal the church a sure death-blow.

Moscow emissary Pozdniakov explained to Bishop Vincentas Brizgys personally that the Catholic clergy must understand the situation and become loyal in a truly positive sense to the new regime. There must be no illusions, he said. What had been accomplished in Russia in 20 years would take only two or three years in Lithuania. There was absolutely no need for seminaries. Why deceive young men and lure them into study for the priesthood, when by ordination time there would be nothing for them to do? Even the Bishop himself, Pozdniakov said, ought to consider what he might be doing in a few years when the people no longer listened to him.[3]

The Communists expected that at least half of Lithuania's priests would be persuaded to leave the priesthood for some "positive" area of activity. With this in mind, the priests were enticed to civilian jobs, but none accepted the offers. One or two were forced to refrain from expressing themselves freely, but these were rare exceptions. The authorities also tried to find priests who would consent to spy on their confreres, but, rather than do so, they chose prison or fled to Germany.

After the abolition of all patriotic and religious societies, the church remained the only place where men of good will could congregate. Aware of this, the Communists organized a close watch on the priests, whom they labelled enemies of the people and exploiters of the working class. These foes of Communism were to be destroyed at any cost—such was the gist of the resolutions passed at Communist party sessions. Towards the end of 1940, J. Paleckis, head of Lithu-

---

[3] *Lietuvių Archyvas* (Kaunas, 1942), I, pp. 61-62.

ania's Communist government, told Herr Hildebrand, a
German journalist, that he had received instructions from
higher authority not to apply any direct pressure on the
clergy. This statement, however, proved to be false, for
shortly afterward there began a direct interference with the
priests' slightest moves.

What the Communists really thought of the clergy and
how they planned to subdue it may be seen from a secret
circular issued by Vice-Commissar Gladkov to all district
chiefs of the NKVD (Secret Police). This communication
was an order to wage war against the "antagonistic acts of
the clergy." All priests, deans, and members of diocesan
Curia were to be kept under formal guard and their activity
to be duly noted. Information about them was to be gathered
through agents—priests and church workers enrolled as
spies. It was necessary to ascertain which priests still maintained contact with the people, especially school children
and lay leaders; upper class pupils were to be used in this
divisive, destructive work. Similar spying was to be done
among those in the religious orders. The circular added that
"some priests were materially unprovided and were waver-
ing in their ideological belief." The requested information
was to be submitted to the Secret Police headquarters by
October 10, 1940.[4]

On January 21, 1941, Gladkov ordered the Secret Police
to submit to him by January 30 a list of clergymen of all
denominations and the extent of the influence of each one
in the political life of his community.[5] This list was needed
for the planned complete extermination of the clergy. This
step, however, because of foreseeable public reaction, was

---

[4] Ibid., pp. 29-31.
[5] Ibid., pp. 33-34.

temporarily postponed until the time when national genocide was to be carried out.

Why genocide? Because the Soviets realized that the Lithuanian nation was almost unanimous in its opposition to the occupation and the attempted communization of its country. The entire people, therefore, according to a fiend-ish plan contrived by the dictators in Moscow, was to be eliminated by physical force.

THE FIRST ARRESTS

Eradication of the Lithuanian people was begun as soon as the Soviets set foot on Lithuanian soil. As early as July 7, 1940, plans were laid for the arrest of 2,000 Lithuanian leaders. These arrests were carried out on the night of July 11. From that time on, arrests did not cease. Prisons were soon overfilled, and new detention facilities had to be pro-vided. Those arrested, after being subjected to various tor-tures, were either shot or exiled to Siberia.

Since the pace of extermination of a people seemed too leisurely, Moscow devised a new plan, which would extin-guish with one sure blow the prevalent anti-Soviet elements. The Russian-appointed Lithuanian Commissar for Home Affairs Guzevičius, on November 28, 1940, issued an order for the registration of members of political parties, employees of state institutions, members of Catholic organizations, for-mer army officers, policemen, foreigners, Polish refugees, clergymen of all denominations, and even philatelists and students of Esperanto! All these supposedly hostile elements —14 categories in all—were designated for liquidation.[6]

---

[6] *Ibid.*, p. 21.

MASS DEPORTATIONS

On the morning of June 15, 1941, in accordance with a minutely detailed plan of USSR Security Deputy Commissar Serov, 34,260 Lithuanian inhabitants—among them the sick, the aged, and children—were packed into freight-cars ordinarily used for shipping livestock and sent on a harrowing journey to undisclosed regions in Russia. Without food and water, and with little air in the suffocatingly crowded cars, many died on the way, some even before they left Lithuanian territory.

Other such deportations were scheduled to follow. According to the category lists made up by Commissar Guzevičius, about 700,000 were to be shipped to Siberia. Only the start of the war with Germany interrupted the execution of the plan.

Among the first deportees were nine Lithuanian priests and a number of Polish refugee priests. Fiften priests were put to death by the retreating Russian soldiers. Eighteen who were in prison at the time were able to escape.

III. UNDER NAZI OCCUPATION

IN THE FIRST DAYS of the Nazi-Soviet war, even before the German troops marched into Lithuania, the entire Lithuanian nation rose against the Russian Communists. Lithuania's independence was declared restored, and a newly-formed provisional government nullified all laws which had been promulgated by the Russian invaders. Seminaries were re-opened, chaplains returned to their posts in prisons and hospitals, and religious instruction in the schools was again made possible. Two months later, however, the German occupational forces dissolved Lithuania's provisional government and reinstated the previous Russian regulations.

The Nazi occupation period, 1941-44, was not an easy one for the Catholic Church. Its schools remained closed. It had no publications. Its property was under the watchful eye of the German occupation authority. In 1942 the Nazis closed the Vilnius Theological Seminary, deported 50 of its seminarians to Germany, and imprisoned about 30 priests. At the same time, they confiscated the convents and forbade the nuns to wear their habit. Thousands of the country's inhabitants were shipped to labor camps in Germany and several thousand, including priests who had given aid to Jews, were sent to concentration camps.

With the approach of the battle front and the threat of a second Soviet invasion, about 60,000 Lithuanians—among them three bishops and 250 priests—withdrew to Germany.

23

IV. THE RUSSIANS RETURN

WHEN THE GERMANS retreated before the victorious Russian armies, the Russians again occupied Lithuania and again began the persecution of the Church—this time with even greater vehemence.

In the autumn of 1945 they resumed mass deportations, which grew in scale until, by 1948-49, they extended over the whole country. The largest of the mass deportations were linked with liquidation of the partisans, who were showing a fierce and unyielding resistance to the invader. Many priests were deported at the same time, accused of aiding or expressing sympathy for the partisans, whom the occupants called "nationalist bandits." This, however, was only a pretext to wipe out the clergy, close more churches, and harass the faithful.

Deportations continued, though reduced in size and limited to certain areas, until the end of 1953.

STORY OF A WITNESS

How the clergy in Lithuania was terrorized may be seen in the following characteristic episode related by a German woman, who with other Germans was then living in Lithuania to escape the near-famine conditions prevalent in the Lithuania Minor area:

> When I reached Lithuania, I was given shelter by the pastor at Pajūris. He was a kind-hearted, charitable

24

priest, respected and loved by everyone. Evidently this did not sit well with the Bolsheviks. Not a day went by that they did not molest him for one reason or another. Why did he light the candles in the church in the evening—as a signal to the partisans, no doubt? Why did he hear confessions? They were particularly incensed when he refused to bury in consecrated ground four Communist and MVD agents liquidated by the partisans.

On the evening of February 6, 1949, the pastor, as was his habit, checked to see that the doors were locked and went to bed. At about midnight I was awakened by a roar of trucks outside. A few minutes later I heard a banging on the door with rifle butts. I dressed hurriedly and ran downstairs. The entire household was already assembled. The pastor was surrounded by twelve agents of the MVD (Secret Police), who were armed with automatic rifles. They were threatening him with fists and cursing him in words that I did not understand. One of the police tore off the small cross the priest was wearing around his neck. Then they ransacked the house. They brought all the books, pictures and church banners, threw everything in a heap, tore and kicked everything about, shouting "Partisans! Bandits!" The pastor watched and didn't say a word. He seemed somewhat pale, but his face showed no sign of fright.

Then they demanded food and drink. When the table was set, they mockingly invited him to join them in "The Last Supper." The pastor did not touch anything. The marauders stuffed themselves with food and liquor and drank "to the pastor's health."

It was dawn when the orgy ended. The pastor was allowed to take a few pieces of clothing and was shoved outside.

Later, from Siberia, he wrote that living conditions were unbearable.[1]

REMOVAL OF THE BISHOPS

Unable to subdue the widespread partisan hostility against them, the Communists demanded that the bishops denounce all resistance to the Soviet administration and that they persuade the partisans to surrender. The bishops' refusal met with stern threats and subsequent arrest by the Secret Police.

The first victim was Vincentas Borisevičius, Bishop of Telšiai, who was arrested on February 3, 1946, and condemned to death after a secret trial in Vilnius in October of the same year. Although several Jewish witnesses, whose lives the Bishop had saved during the Nazi occupation, testified on his behalf, his fate was determined by the charge that he had been a "bourgeois national leader." When the judge, after announcing the sentence, boasted tauntingly, "It is we who are the victors," the Bishop calmly replied, "Your hour of victory is brief. The future is mine. Christ will be victorious, just as my Lithuania will be victorious."

Before the year's end, his auxiliary, Bishop Pranas Ramanauskas, was also arrested and deported to Siberia. At about the same time Bishop Teofilius Matulionis of Kaišiadorys and Archbishop Mečislovas Reinys of Vilnius were deported to a Siberian labor camp. Archbishop Reinys perished while in prison at Vladimir, November 8, 1953. By 1947 Lithuania was left with a single bishop, Kazimieras Paltarokas, in the diocese of Panevėžys. He died in Vilnius on January 3, 1958.

---

[1] From a statement by Frau X, recorded verbatim upon her return to her home near Koenigsberg.

INTERFERENCE WITH SEMINARIES

Having occupied Lithuania for the second time, the Russian Communists again closed the theological seminaries at Telšiai and Vilkaviškis. (The Vilnius seminary had remained closed since the Soviet occupation in 1939.) This left only the Kaunas seminary open. The number of students, however, was restricted to 150. This number was steadily reduced, until by 1964 only five new entrants, of a total of 25 seminarians, were being accepted. A special government permit, difficult to obtain, is now required for enrollment. Attempts have been made by the government to infiltrate the seminary student body with Communists, and there is much interference with the internal affairs of the institution. The seminarians are subjected to frequent search, and many professors and members of the administrative staff have been deported to Siberia.

RELIGIOUS ORDERS DISBANDED

In 1947 the last of the convents and monasteries were closed and their religious communities dispersed. All monastic institutions were outlawed, and any person discovered to be a member of one faced imprisonment or deportation.

V. A BREATHING SPELL

AFTER STALIN'S DEATH on March 5, 1953, the religious situation took a slight turn for the better. Stalin's successor,
Khrushchev, created a sensation when, on November 10,
1954, he admitted that brutal anti-religious assaults had been
inflicted upon priests and the faithful, and that ignorant
propagandists had outrageously violated the people's feelings. All this, a decree of the party's Central Committee
said, must be changed. In the future, the fight against religion must be conducted on a purely ideological basis by
persons especially trained for the purpose.[1]

This change in policy was explained in the Lithuanian
Communist Party organ *Tiesa* (Aug. 10, 1955) as follows:

> There are many collective farmers and workers in
> our republic who, while engaged in productive work
> and conscientiously performing their duties of citizen-
> ship, are still influenced by religious beliefs. Our party
> teaches us to be more considerate in our dealings with
> these people. It would be foolish and harmful to treat
> them with suspicion solely because of their religious be-
> liefs, which are merely a residue of the past. Our strug-
> gle with religious superstitions must now be viewed as
> a struggle of the ideological, scientific, materialistic con-
> cept against the unscientific and religious point of view.

RELIGION FREELY DISCUSSED

The ideological warfare against religion advocated by

---

[1] *Pravda* (Moscow), November 10, 1954.

Khrushchev was subject to various interpretations. It was difficult for a while to settle on the precise line of action to follow. As a result of this confusion, there appeared in Communist newspapers in 1956 actual discussions of religious questions. This opened the way for the faithful to express publicly, even if guardedly, their religious convictions.

For example, a candidate of the LSSR Academy of Science wrote in carefully chosen words:

> Religious belief does not necessarily make bad collective farmers, bad workers, or generally inept citizens of our socialist country. Surely all of us are acquainted with religious people who are industrious, conscientious, and capable in the performance of their duties. These persons could undoubtedly attain even better results, greater accomplishments, if they did not poison their consciousness with religious superstitions.[2]

L. Drotvinas, a product of the Soviet system of education, had the following interesting arguments in defense of religion:

> We must not forget that, in the course of history, religion has played a double role: art—painting, music, architecture—owes much to religion; at the same time religion has helped to exploit people and to repress their initiative in the struggle for freedom, though in this respect we must recall that we always had clergymen who appeared on the scene as leaders of the masses in their battle for freedom. Thus the positive significance of religion today is that many of our older generation have been brought up under certain religious precepts: Do not steal; do not lie, etc. On the other

---

[2] *Tiesa* (Vilnius), October 21, 1956.

hand, we have many who, though irreligious, are not necessarily immoral.

Religion is no obstacle to an educated man. Present-day religion is so modernized and makes so many allowances that one cannot say that it hinders the development of science, engineering, or art. The technical and scientific progress of mankind can be clearly seen, even in countries where religion has a certain legal status, where scientists are religious men. Conversely, art, especially painting, when we compare it to that of previous centuries, has sunk to a much lower level, even though the 20th century is noticeably more godless.

Religion does not repress a worker's or a farmer's initiative, for it does not urge him to work badly or not to work at all. Holy days and religious services, with their music, hymns, ceremony, and glitter, are a pleasant habit, especially for the older generation, and have not been replaced—nor can they be replaced— by cinema or other cultural entertainment, of which there is too little and which is not always cultural.

In the olden days, the few atheists in Lithuania led exemplary lives and merely contended with their state-protected clerical adversaries. Among present-day atheists we find many unsavory, loose-living individuals. So it is impossible to say who is better: the person who goes to church or the one who frequents the barroom. This question is far too complex to be solved easily . . .

A religious fanatic and his anti-religious opposite are equally stupid . . .[3]

This was the last article written in *defense* of religion, for it was immediately recognized that the subject was being discussed too freely. Under Moscow's new instructions, religion was again to be attacked, scoffed at, ridiculed.

---

[3] *Tiesa*, December 11, 1956.

AMNESTIES

On February 27, 1953, and September 17, 1955, amnesty was granted to some prisoners in Siberia. This enabled about 35,000 of about 300,000 deportees to return to Lithuania. Others, although released from hard labor, were forced to remain in Russia, most of them in Asiatic areas. About 130 priests came back to Lithuania, a few remaining voluntarily with the exiles to minister to their spiritual needs.

Bishops Matulionis and Ramanauskas were among those who returned, but they were not allowed to administer their dioceses or communicate with their clergy or the laity. They had to reside where directed: Archbishop Matulionis in Še duva (died August 20, 1963), Bishop Ramanauskas in Švėkšna (died October 15, 1959).

Those who returned from Siberia were never completely rehabilitated. Instead, their alleged crimes are continually harped on in the press.

On September 11, 1955, two new Rome appointed bish ops, Julijonas Steponavičius and Petras Maželis, were con secrated. The former has never been permitted by the Communist regime to perform administrative duties. Bishop Vincentas Slatkevičius, consecrated on September 25, 1957, is also under severe government restrictions; he is forbidden even to issue a pastoral letter. On December 5, 1965, Mon signor Juozas Labukas Matulaitis was consecrated in Rome to head the archdiocese of Kaunas and the diocese of Vil kaviškis.

VI. THE STRUGGLE RENEWED

RECOGNIZING THE CHURCH'S STRENGTH

THE COMPARATIVELY RELAXED state of affairs was brief. It was frightening to the Communist leaders that a slight lessening of pressure had revealed that the Lithuanian people were still deeply religious. Even some Party members and those in the *Komsomol* (Young Communist League) were found to be indulging in religious practices. It was decided, therefore, to launch a most powerful offensive to wipe out every trace of religion in the country. This was to be accomplished concurrently with the building of the Communist society.

The main implement of attack would be unlimited moral pressure, since physical terror seemed only to strengthen and unify the faithful. What particularly angered the Communists was the evidence that, although the underground partisan resistance had been checked, the collective farm system had been forced upon the people and the so-called bourgeois class had been exterminated, the Church remained a national and spiritual center of resistance.

The Church was the chief obstacle in the way of Moscow's plans to merge and submerge little Lithuania into the giant Soviet empire. It was the Church, said the Communists, which fused the national and religious viewpoints into a single ideological battlefront.

"The Church and its priests," wrote a Communist journalist, "have for centuries enmeshed the populace in religious cobwebs, which now are difficult to break."[1]

---

[1] *Komunistas* (Vilnius), September, 1960.

"Religion," we read in another evaluation, "is the most vital and the most harmful remnant of the past. It inhibits a large segment of the Soviet population from actively joining in the building of Communism."[2]

ATHEISTIC PROPAGANDA

The Communists attach the utmost importance to propaganda. An article in the daily *Tiesa* (August 19, 1956) enumerates some specific points:

> To spread scientific-atheistic propaganda we must employ all means: lectures, reports, the press, radio, cinema, and the theatre. For this unusually important work we must enroll the best party propagandists, men of science, Soviet intellectuals and agriculture specialists. It is imperative that lectures be given in every factory, office and farm, in order that the immortal ideas of Marxism and Leninism spread enlightenment among the workers.

At a meeting called in 1962 by the editors of the magazine *Komunistas* it was agreed among the party chiefs, professors, and newspaper editors present that propaganda for atheism must consist of: (1) an "unmasking" of religion and the exposure of the "superstitions" which prevent the people from involvement in "life's lofty reality"; and (2) arming of the workers with information which is scientific and more closely related to social, economic, and political problems.

In order to achieve the scientific approach, the Communist Party Secretary A. Barkauskas, at the party's Central Committee meeting held in Vilnius, February 12-13, 1963, presented the following guide lines:

---

[2] *Sovietskaja Litva* (Vilnius), September 15, 1954.

Atheistic education of the masses must continue in full force, even though a sizable portion of the workers have shaken off their religious habits. Formation of materialistic philosophy must be the primary concern of all leading organizations and party committees. The scientific-atheistic propaganda must reach every stratum of the population and be appropriate to each group's age, level of education, and interests.

Without exception, all graduates of secondary and technical schools and universities must be deeply convinced and active atheists.

Newspapers must dwell extensively on atheistic topics. Using concrete examples from life as well as artistic material, our press must reveal the utter incompatibility between the reality of life and religious superstitions . . . and must fight against religion as an anti-scientific ideology. Radio and television should also improve their work in this direction.

In literary works, whatever the theme being developed, must run a red thread of atheistic anti-clericalism.

The Committee for Higher Education and Specialized Secondary Schools, as well as the Academy of Arts and Sciences, must in all seriousness concern themselves with the direction and coordination of scientific research of atheism.

Institutions of higher learning must increase their efforts in this respect. The course in Elements of Scientific Atheism must be utilized more effectively. Additional possibilities for the preparation of atheists can be found in student clubs, special class assignments and various group projects. It is extremely important that the students themselves actively participate in the propaganda work, especially while on vacation or when engaged in productive employment between school terms.

Scientifically atheistic education of the inhabitants, especially the youth, is the party's ideological task. It is a matter of honor and duty for every Party member,

Communist youth worker, union member, farm leader, and intellectual. Each must work in his own field with the best available means.[3]

THE PLAN IN OPERATION

To saturate the country with atheistic propaganda, special agitator groups were formed of professors, teachers, doctors, scientists, writers, artists, newspapermen. By 1960 there were 779 such groups. In Kaunas alone 3,000 persons were engaged in this work. In 1962 the country's leading anti-religious organization had over 18,000 members, of whom 13,000 were active in farms and villages. In the course of one year this army of propagandists was responsible for giving 100,000 lectures before a combined audience of 6,000,000.[4]

For a wider dissemination of the doctrine of atheism, small atheist units were formed in every educational institution, industrial plant and farm, and wherever there was a larger group of workers. In 1962 Šiauliai had 55 of these units with more than 1,000 members and a school for group leaders; in Vilnius there were 70 units.[5]

Exultation was expressed in the columns of *Tiesa* (May 28, 1963) over the activity of 11 newly-formed atheist groups on the collective farms of the district of Radviliškis, whose first atheist rally in May, 1963, at Šeduva, was said to have drawn 250 enthusiastic delegates and featured an "interesting" atheistic exhibit.

---

[3] *Tiesa*, February 16, 1963.

[4] From a report given at an anti-religious propaganda conference by Prof. K. Baršauskas, president of the Society for Dissemination of Political and Scientific Information, Kaunas, April 13-14, 1962. See *Eltos Informacijos*, April 28, 1962, and *Tiesa*, April 15, 1962.

[5] *Tiesa*, February 16, 1963.

EDUCATION OF THE WORKERS

Factory workers are an important target for atheistic indoctrination. A single automobile-brake factory at Panevėžys has an atheist unit of 250 members. The extent of their efforts in this sphere is notable. Bi-weekly discussions are held on such subjects as "How Man Created God" and "How We Stopped Believing in God." Wall newspapers carry the atheist message in every factory department. The factory has a library of atheistic literature and an atheist school attended by 32 workers. An expansion of these activities beyond the bounds of the factory is planned.[6]

At a meeting of the Communist party activists in August 1963, S. Jurgaitis, leader of the Panevėžys atheists, reported that in the schools and business concerns of his city there were 41 atheist groups with 1,700 militant members.[7]

MUCH IS EXPECTED OF YOUTH

Members of the Young Communist League are expected to show special zeal in the propagation of atheism. Following Moscow's instructions, they must fight "religious superstition," explain to the workers the phenomena of nature, and popularize the achievements in astronomy, biology, chemistry, physics, medicine. They should direct all atheistic endeavor in schools, businesses, factories, and farms. They must see that organization members refrain from church-going and all religious practices. They must obstruct the observance of holy days and divert these occasions to the League's purposes.

---

[6] *Tiesa,* July 13, 1963.
[7] *Lietuvių Religinė Informacija* (New York), August 31, 1963.

PROFESSORS NOT EXCLUDED

The teaching of atheism is not to be confined to the classroom. Professors must extend their atheistic missionary effort even to small towns and collective farms. In the town of Gruzdžiai, for example, weekly lectures and discussions on the senselessness of religion are conducted by professors of Šiauliai Pedagogical Institute.[8]

WRITERS ENGAGED IN THE CAUSE

The power of the printed word in the anti-religious campaign is not overlooked. Newspapers are full of articles deriding religion and the faithful. Reporters vie with one another in their effort to prove the harmfulness of religion and to expose the "crimes of the clergy." Literary journals are similarly anti-religious in content. At Vilnius, on October 3-4, 1963, there was held a seminar on atheism for journalists of all three Soviet-occupied Baltic States, with about 100 journalists present.[9]

Writers of novels and other literary works also tread the same anti-God path, knowing that the best reviews invariably go to books on anti-religious themes. Prizes are given for the best anti-religious plays submitted during special contests. To supply the atheist groups with material for their entertainment programs, a two-volume collection of satire and humor was published, since these have been recognized as effective weapons.[10]

A CALL ON THE MEDICAL PROFESSION

An important role is assigned to doctors, both practicing physicians and medical school faculty members. Their lec-

---

[8] *Valstiečių Laikraštis* (Vilnius), October 27, 1963.
[9] *Tiesa,* October 5, 1963.
[10] *Lietuvių Religinė Informacija,* April 30, 1963.

tures must not only inform the listeners on developments in the field of medicine, but also help to influence the formation of a materialistic point of view. In the course of explaining various natural phenomena the lecturer has an opportunity to "unmask the falsity of non-scientific, idealistic beliefs" and to "prove" how irreconcilable religion is with the science of medicine. Moreover, church-instilled "notions" about the immortality of the soul can be effectively dispelled by scientifically-based discourse on the origin of matter, the evolution of life, and other scientific subjects.

Complying with these directives, Dr. V. Kantauskas, bacteriologist, and Dr. V. Murauskas, professor at the Institute of Medicine, set out to prove that "in present-day religion there are many unhygienic practices, such as kissing of the crucifix, the relics, and the priest's hand, dipping of the fingers in holy water, etc. To give added weight to this argument, a microbiological laboratory made bacteriological tests in the Kaunas Cathedral and other churches and came up with the finding that the holy water was polluted from unclean fingers being dipped in it; that the spots where the crucifix is kissed were swarming with microorganisms which can cause angina pectoris, erysipelas, scarlet fever, abscesses, septemia, heart ailments, and other diseases.

In view of this "incontestable evidence," the doctors, as "guardians of health and citizen-atheists," were urged by the press to expose the senselessness of "religious superstitions" and the damage they do to health. Doctors in village dispensaries were of prime importance in this work. Country doctors, too, were to strive to frighten their farmer patients from going to church by explaining to them how easily infectious diseases could be contracted by the use of holy water and kissing the cross.[11] Doctors were instructed to travel through the countryside, singly or in groups, preaching atheism.

In a Vilnius radio broadcast on March 19, 1963, Dr. J. Kanapeckas discussed the work of a newly-organized group of atheist doctors in the town of Rokiškis, where seven doctors—all from the local hospital—spoke at their specially arranged gathering and sought to convince the audience that medicine must battle "religious superstition." On a tour of neighboring towns by this same group, one surgeon stated that, whereas ten years ago 30 to 50 per cent of hospital patients made the sign of the cross before going on the operating table, this practice was now rarely seen, and that this fact showed how weak religious belief had become.[12]

Though the doctors make every effort to comply with their extra-curricular assignment—to inflict injury on the spiritual being of a person—the results are not noteworthy. Not all doctors are enthusiastic about a chore completely unrelated to their medical practice. They are continually prodded and showered with "enlightenment" through publications and doctors' seminars. One seminar, held in Vilnius in June, 1963, was attended by more than 200 doctors.[13] Doctors are reprimanded in the press for permitting secret baptism of infants in clinics and for tolerating visits of the clergy in hospitals.[14]

Appealing to people's self-interest, Dr. Vaičiuvėnas, in his book, *Man and the Superstitions of Religion,* argues that a person who accepts disease as God-sent punishment weakens his powers of resistance and impedes recovery.

---

[11] *Tiesa,* July 26, 1961.
[12] *Lietuvių Religinė Informacija,* March 31, 1963.
[13] *Lietuvių Religinė Informacija,* August 30, 1963.
[14] *Tiesa,* May 30, 1963.

FORMER PRIESTS ARE USED

A number of former priests, such as Stasys Markonis and Dorotiejus Bazčastnas—the latter, for his immoral behavior, had been defrocked in Rome and came back to Lithuania as a "martyr"—are among the more active anti-religious propagandists.

One who is considered a real prize for his prolific activity is Jonas Ragauskas, who serves his Communist masters with a continuous flood of books, articles, lectures, and radio talks, travelling from one end of Lithuania to the other. After one of his lectures in Kaunas, during the usual question-and-answer period, one young girl handed in a slip of paper with the following inquiry: "You, who once served God under oath, have now trampled everything under your feet, have sold yourself to the Communists, and serve the devil. How do you justify this?" Since all inquiries were carefully screened by his secretary, this question remained unanswered.[15]

Another time, in Šakiai, when Ragauskas walked into the lecture hall, his audience of collective farmers, who had been driven there by force, knelt and began singing the hymn "Let Us Fall On Our Knees." To the astonished Ragauskas they explained, "We thought, Father, that you have come to hold services for us." Such is the reaction this ex-priest's activity awakens in most people.[16] They look upon such unfortunate victims of Communism with more pity than anger.

ALL MUST BE ACTIVE ATHEISTS

Nowadays it is not enough to be a passive listener at

---

15 *Eltos Informacijos* (Reutlingen), March 4, 1961.
16 *Elta Press* (Rome), December, 1963.

lectures on atheism. All government employees, teachers, and doctors are bluntly warned that if they do not wish to lose their positions, they must publicly declare their atheism.

How can one be a good doctor, goes the argument, if he believes in God and thus denies Darwin's theory of the origin of man and the Marxist-Leninist teachings about the beginning of the world? Such a doctor obviously has doubts about the healing qualities of medicine. Similarly, a teacher is unable to mold his students into real Communists if he himself is entrapped in "religious superstitions." Such characters are fit to be street cleaners, not doctors or teachers.

Thus it is understandable that the Communist press is full of public confessions and disavowals of any religious faith. In the newspaper *Tiesa* (The Truth) there is a section called "My Path to Atheism," devoted entirely to these confessions.

Students, too, make their public confessions. In *Komjaunimo Tiesa* (Communist Youth Truth), October 25, 1963, a girl student wrote: "I need no gods or saints. I believe only in the working man."

In the monthly *Mokslas ir Gyvenimas* (Science and Life), April, 1959, eminent writers contribute such articles as "The Evolution of My Philosophy," "How I Stopped Believing in God," and others.

At a plenary meeting of Lithuania's Communist Party Central Committee in Vilnius, February 12-13, 1963, Party Secretary A. Barkauskas stressed personal example as a particularly convincing method of indoctrination. Soon after, on March 5, a farmer and a teacher were heard on the radio describing how they had found their way to atheism and shaken off religious belief for all time.

INDIVIDUAL ATTENTION

Despite the efforts of the atheists, a woman factory worker openly continued to practice her religion. The factory management was loath to dismiss her; a specialist in her work, she was irreplaceable.

A different approach was devised. One day she received a surprise visit from her brother, who lived and worked in another city.

"I have an assignment," he told her. "I must dissuade you from going to church."

"Your efforts are in vain," she replied sharply. "I have my beliefs and I am not going to give them up."

"Now wait," explained the brother, "I was told that if I do not convince you I will lose my job and face Siberia. I have a family. What is going to happen to them? If you want to ruin me, then stick to your old practices."

In the end, out of pity for her brother, the woman ceased attending church. This is but one example of the methods employed to "convert" people to atheism.

"PEOPLE'S UNIVERSITIES"

To achieve the desired reeducation of the rural population, the Communists constantly experiment with new measures. A comparatively recent invention is that of "People's Universities" on collective farms. In 1960, in the Panevėžys district, for example, there were two such institutions, while two years later there were seven, with a Department of Atheism operating in each. In 1963, at one of these training centers in the village of Staniūnai there were 150 persons taking the course in atheism; the instructors were prominent atheists from the city of Panevėžys. Films, drawings, photographs, and stage presentations were used to illustrate the lectures. Seminars were held to acquaint the students with books on atheism.[17]

Students at Kėdainiai had the privilege of joining an excursion to Leningrad's Museum of the History of Religion and Atheism. In 1963 there were 49 who completed the atheism course at Kėdainiai, and all immediately embarked on atheistic work. Authorities express gratification that such courses throughout the country prepare a substantial number of militant atheists.[18]

Almost every city has its Atheists' House. Here members are divided into sections and apply themselves to specific assignments: delivering lectures, distributing atheistic litera-ture, writing newspaper articles, arranging question-and-answer sessions, organizing atheist circles in schools, training new propagandists and cultivating relations with similar Atheist Houses in the USSR, source of additional guidance. These centers are also used for atheistic trials and atheistic christenings and weddings.

Although the Society for the Propagation of Political and Scientific Information, a subsidiary of a Moscow organi-zation, had a wide network of branches in Lithuania, espe-cially in the villages, and despite numerous other atheist groups, schools, and centers, the results of their efforts were not outstanding. To give atheistic work greater focus and centralized direction, the end of 1962 saw the formation in Vilnius of a Soviet Council of Atheistic Propaganda. This super-planning and coordinating agency consists of scientists, teachers, and party representatives of the press, radio, and television. Similarly, every city and district has its own coun-

---

[17] *Komjaunimo Tiesa* (Vilnius), May 15, 1963.
[18] *Lietuvių Religinė Informacija*, May 31, 1963.

cil of distinguished local atheists. At the University of Vilnius, the Students' Council "offers a helping hand" in propaganda work among students, lecturers, and the general public.

Although the campaign against religion in Lithuania appears to be highly developed, to Moscow it is ever insufficient in scope. Thus there constantly emanate from the Soviet capital new exhortations, new directions how to extend and intensify this fight. Following the Communist Party Central Committee's plenary meeting in Moscow, June 18-21, 1963, the Lithuanian Communist press evidenced renewed emphasis on the battle against religion.

"It is inconceivable," wrote the magazine *Mokslas ir Gyvenimas* (July, 1963), "that we can evolve a scientific viewpoint and a Communist morality without waging war against religious ideology. Religion is the chief antagonist of the Communist-scientific concept in this country, one of the worn-out notions from which large segments of the population have not yet freed themselves. . . . We must counter religion by militant, aggressive, scientific-atheistic propaganda."

Religion, we are told, is not only "the opium of the masses," as Marx maintained, but "a virulent growth, which has deeply embedded its roots into people's consciousness."[19] It is "a snake whose teeth must be drawn out. We must dig our way under the foundations of religion to the very depths of its hypocrisy."[20]

ATHEISTIC PRESS

The entire Communist press is enlisted in the spreading of atheistic propaganda. Every newspaper and magazine con-

[19] *Valstiečių Laikraštis*, October 9, 1963.
[20] *Tiesa*, January 26, 1963.

tains articles ridiculing religion, the faithful, and the clergy. The magazine *Mokslas ir Gyvenimas,* which began publication in 1957, is specifically dedicated to the advancement of atheism. Every issue has one or more anti-religious articles. The stories and sketches have an anti-religious bias.

Publication of atheistic books and pamphlets—original works and translations—is a major endeavor. The Lithuanian Communist Party Secretary A. Sniečkus revealed in 1949 that the annual output of newspapers and periodicals which expose "the reactionary activity of the Catholic clergy" was 650,000 copies. A group of translators in Vilnius is responsible for making available some of the ugliest anti-religious literature, of Russian and other foreign authorship.

Between 1945 and 1962, a total of 235 books on atheistic subjects were published, with a grand total of copies printed reaching 1,154,000. In the period of January-November, 1963, 30 atheistic works—403,000 copies—rolled off the printing presses. About 30 more atheistic books were planned for 1964 publication.

The books serve various purposes. Some are textbooks for propagandists; others are meant for mass consumption. A considerable portion aims to "unmask the criminal activities" of the clergy. Lest the public overlook some of this literature, special book fairs are organized.

One such event in Kaunas was described in a Vilnius radio account on October 7, 1954, as containing more than 3,000 books and brochures on anti-religious topics in various languages and a special section of drawings and photographs dealing with cult practices around the world. The Vatican and the Catholic Church were depicted as "trusty agents of imperialism." One section of the fair displayed literature which "unmasks" the popes of Rome. Here the visitor found Jaroslav Galan's book, *The Father of Darkness and the Vatican without the Mask*. One showcase displayed the book, *The Reactionary Clergy—Eternal Foe of the Lithuanian People* by Prof. Juozas Žiugžda. Another, by Prof. Paulius Pakarklis, was *The Popes—Enemies of the Lithuanian Nation*.

It is evident that the purpose of these book exhibits is to bring the vast collection of atheistic literature to the attention of the general public and to spread Communist slander and incrimination of the church and its clergy.

RADIO

Radio is widely used as a medium for the advancement of atheism. Vilnius radio regularly devotes certain hours to atheistic indoctrination. The weekly Thursday program of the Atheists' Club answers questions on such religious topics as: "Whence Came Christianity?"; "Why the Whole World Observes Sunday as a Holy Day"; "Is Science Compatible with Religion?"

On the same Vilnius radio one can often hear reports about Lithuania's priests, their "nationalist" actions during the Nazi occupation, and their participation in "shooting of innocent people." Satiric narratives deride the clergy and the faithful.

A program of talks for school pupils might discuss at length the question of who created man and then arrives at the customary Communist answer that man has deviated from the ape.[21]

---

[21] See *Lietuvių Religinė Informacija*, January 26, 1963.

FILM FARE

Communist films offer pseudo-scientific explanations of the creation of the world, the essence of life, etc. One film, *The Turkey,* in its attempt to portray saints and miracles as nauseously ridiculous, was so repulsive that even the Communists admitted that the film's ugliness can only drive the faithful further from atheism.

The film *In the Shadow of the Cross,* produced in 1961, was intended to be an indictment of the whole religious morality and its defenders. The opening scene shows the vaulted interior of a church and the praying congregation. The film ends with the shout, "Draw back and leave these walls that reek with chill."[22] The film maliciously falsifies the facts, showing Archbishop Skvireckas of Kaunas thanking the Nazis for the massacre of thousands of people and the burning of towns and villages. The film attempts to prove that priests were not only collaborators of the Nazi plunderers, but also blood-thirsty characters.[23]

A documentary film, *The Black Procession,* shows actual scenes of the 1962 celebrations of the feasts of the Blessed Virgin at Šiluva and Žemaičių Kalvarija, but the scenes are interspersed with dramatized sequences, music, and the producers' own perverted explanations, which describe the "backwardness" of religious faith, create doubt in miracles, and stir up hatred of the clergy.

To supplement the locally-made product, anti-religious films are also imported from other countries. One such film that reached the Lithuanian screen in April, 1963, is of Moldavian origin and features a leader of Jehovah's Witnesses in the role of a U.S. spy and murderer.

---

22 *Komjaunimo Tiesa,* February 9, 1962.
23 *Tiesa,* February 9, 1962.

TELEVISION

Vilnius television makes its contribution to the required enlightenment with pictures and sketches of the "reactionary clergy." Loathsome caricatures, made by Art Institute students, try to show the clergy's close association with the "national bourgeoisie," "national bandits" (partisans), and the like. The Vatican is depicted as "a nest of obscurantism and an ally of the imperialists."

MUSEUMS

Heretofore, atheistic museums in various localities have not been distinguished for their wealth of exhibits. But Vilnius' new Central Museum of Atheism, established in 1962 in the Church of St. Casimir, which had been closed, is said to be the first of its kind in the Baltic countries. For its collection, churches all over Lithuania are being divested of their more notable paintings and devotional articles. From the closed church of Senoji Žagarė they have removed the uncorrupted body of Venerable Barbara, which the populace worships as a saint. This will be used as a museum item exposing "priestly fraud." Under the direction of an ex-priest, the museum is responsible for organizing travelling exhibits, helping to set up local atheist centers and spreading the atheist movement by other means. The museum also has an atheistic library.

Miniature museums, called Atheist Rooms, are being installed in district centers. One such Room in Raseiniai has four sections: "Šiluva" (the site of the apparition of Our Lady in 1608), "The Dominicans at Raseiniai," "The True Image of the Church," and "The Absurdity of Religion."[24] This is in line with the express goal—to propagate the "scientific"—atheistic thought. Many local museums throughout Lithuania now boast of having installed such exhibits.

THE THEATRE

The stage, too, is a force in anti-religious propaganda. Among the many atheistic dramas in use are *The Divine Comedy* by J. Stokas, which mocks the biblical interpretation of the creation of the world; *At the Gate of Heaven*, *The Problem of Heaven*, *Miracles Without Miracles*, *The Thorn*, *In the Shadow of the Cross*, and *The Lord God's Guests*. There is also an atheistic opera, *A City of the Sun*.[25]

The services of "agit-brigades" are fully made use of in propaganda work. "By short stage sketches, sprightly couplets, improvisations . . . and poems, they rip off the reactionary clergy's mask."[26]

EXHIBITS

At the Kaunas Historical Museum, near the end of 1962, an exhibit titled *The Truth about Religion* was installed. It consisted of the following sections: "Reactionary Religious Sects," "The Morality of the Servants of God," "New Traditions," "Communistic Morality," "The Conquest of the Cosmos," and "Light Conquers All."[27]

In February, 1963, the Vilnius Museum of Natural Resources opened an exhibit of painting, sculpture, and photography by so-called progressive artists, who had made

24 *Tiesa*, February 8, 1962; April 15, 1962.
25 *Eltos Informacijos*, September 14, 1963.
26 *Tiesa*, April 28, 1962.
27 *Pergalė* (Vilnius), December, 1962.

their initial appearance in their respective fields during the years of Lithuania's independence. Their works were now intended to expose "the truth about the dark deeds of the churchly mob through the ages."[28]

In March, 1963, in the Library of Science at Vilnius University, an exhibit of atheistic literature was opened. Its theme was "Marxism and Leninism on Religion." In addi-tion to a large collection of world literature on atheistic sub-jects, there were quite a few publications on religious-philo-sophical currents in the free world. In a separate section, the Vatican is depicted as "the worst enemy of learning and progress."[29]

Anti-religious exhibits have begun to appear more fre-quently in the outlying rural areas. An exhibit at Kupiškis in 1962 displayed not only "Items of the Inquisition," but also "The Threats of Pope John XXIII." Two of the sections were called "Religion in the Service of Imperialism" and "Religion, a Source of Personal Aggrandizement."[30]

Former religious institutions are likely sites for atheistic exhibits. Kretinga, for example, which had been a center for Lithuania's Franciscan Fathers since 1602 (until the Soviets destroyed the monastery in 1944 and dispersed or killed the Franciscans), with schools, a home for the aged, and a publishing plant, was to house a permanent exhibit dealing with the Franciscans' "reactionary undertakings" and the "crafty means employed to keep the people in ignorance."[31]

A similar fate has befallen the Marian Fathers in Mari-jampolė. In the city where the Marians had conducted a

---

[28] *Eltos Informacijos,* March 2, 1963.
[29] *Lietuvių Religinė Informacija,* March 30, 1963.
[30] *Tiesa,* September 18, 1962.
[31] *Lietuvių Religinė Informacija,* August 31, 1963.

secondary school, printed religious books and newspapers, established a valuable library, and were known for their exemplary pastoral labors among the faithful, an atheist center's permanent exhibit now attempts to show the Marians to have been immoral, greedy pursuers of wealth and exploiters of the working people.[32]

---

[32] See *Valstiečių Laikraštis*, February 18, 1962.

VII. THE ATHEISTS' SPECIAL TARGETS

THE COMMUNISTS have come to the realization that to convert the older generation to atheistic ideology is well nigh
impossible. The centuries-old influence of the Catholic
Church is too deeply entrenched. The emphasis, therefore,
must be laid on the young.

The Communist Party's Central Committee's seventh
plenary session, December 3-4, 1958, had an agenda of only
one item—the strengthening of political and ideological propaganda among school children. New instructions were issued
to teachers for spreading anti-religious propaganda. The
Party and the Communist Youth organization were author-
ized to supervise the teachers' compliance with the new
orders.

Soon after this session, the following article appeared in
a teachers' periodical:[1]

> One of the most important tasks of a teacher is to
> implant in the child a materialistic outlook on life. Much
> can be accomplished by teachers of biology, physics,
> chemistry, history, and literature . . . They must show
> by convincing facts and examples how priests tried to
> distort scientific truths and used them as a means to
> keep the people in ignorance. They must show the pu-
> pils the irreconcilability of science and religion, and
> religion's reactionary role in the advancement of science.
> Teachers can find material for discussion in history

---

[1] *Tarybinis Mokytojas* (Vilnius), December 21, 1958.

books, where religion is often mentioned, for through-out history the Catholic Church has played a most reactionary role. One cannot ignore the politics of the present-day Vatican. Much atheistic material is also available to the teacher of Lithuanian literature. It is not enough, however, to rely on one or two works in analyzing the reactionary position of the Church and its priests. This material must be brought into a rela-tionship with current events. Religion must be exposed to its very roots, so that it will be clearly seen how the servants of religion have always deceived the people, kept them in the dark and encouraged abject submis-siveness to their exploiters.

Teachers of music and art can be very helpful in this program of atheistic education as they discuss the lives of famous artists. Physical training teachers also cannot be excused from taking part in this work.

Soon after receiving these directives, many teachers re-vealed through newspaper columns how they were complying with the new instructions. When teaching Roman history, for example, the origin of "the legend" of Jesus is explained. In Medieval history one discusses how Christianity attained its position of power in the world and the negative role it played in the development of mankind. Referring to individ-ual rulers, one points out their political machinations and the assistance they received from the Church in the attainment of their predatory ambitions. In the physical geography class, when dealing with the subject of mineral springs, a scientific explanation of their origin disposes of the miraculous heal-ing attributes which the priests often give the springs. When delving into the formation of the seas and the oceans, the pupils are taught that the waters were formed quite nat-urally, without any intervention from a "heavenly Creator."

These newspaper reports serve a dual purpose: the

teacher receives recognition that he or she is a reliable atheist, and the readers are encouraged by cited examples to do
likewise.

Yet there are some who complain that atheistic teaching
is not easy. There are frequent occasions when, after listen-
ing to a teacher's lengthy explanation, a pupil will ask why
religion is being persecuted. The teacher is then obliged to
begin his explanation all over again. It is particularly difficult for a teacher to give a satisfactory answer to such a
question as, "Why have all religions throughout the ages
expressed belief in the soul and its immortality?"

After Soviet Premier Khrushchev underlined at the
22nd Congress of the Communist Party the need for "a
logical, well-planned system of atheistic education, which
would reach every stratum of the population and would
serve as a barrier against the spread of religious ideas, especially among children and our young people," it was re-
solved that in Lithuania, too, the schools must produce
confirmed atheists. The 1962-63 school year was to be the
year for the realization of this objective.[2]

The Institute for the Advancement of Teachers prepared
a detailed outline of topics to be covered and procedures
to be followed in Grades 5 through 11. The methodology
took note of three separate areas of atheistic training: instruction in the school; the pupils' atheistic activity outside; the
atheistic approach to religious children. The courses included
the following subject matter:

Grade 5: The origin of religious belief. The origin of
angels and devils. Could a God create the world? Man
created God, and not God man. The Bible, a collection

---

[2] See Tarybinė Mokykla (Vilnius), August, 1962.

of legends and fables. What history says about Christ. Belief in a life hereafter. Why we must fight against religious superstition.

Grade 6: Do prayers help? The origin and absurdity of baptism. Does confession improve a person? Why has the church invented heaven, purgatory, and hell? How saints come into being. Why miracles are needed. Religious feast-days and their origin. Indulgences—a source of personal profit for the priests.

Grade 7: The inquisition against science. The image of the missionary. Religious orders—disseminators of ignorance. Reactionary work of the Church in Lithuania. The Vatican—a bulwark of capitalism. The Communist Party's view of religion. The incompatibility of religious belief with the building of Communism.

Grade 8: Science vs. religion. Noted educators who battled with religion. The new tactics of the church. Science and religion on the origin of life. Medicine and religion. Man and the cosmos.

Grade 9: Religion, its origin and essence.

Grade 10: The Catholic Church, an ally of the exploiters.

Grade 11: The Vatican and U.S. imperialism. The Church—promoter of nationalistic fossils.[3]

A new course in Basic Principles of Social Science was introduced in Lithuania's secondary schools in 1963. Classes meet four times weekly and explore such subjects as: Marxism-Leninism; the Theory of Communism; Socialism—the First Phase of Communism; Gradual Transformation of Socialism into Communism; the 20th Century—the Age of Communism's Victory. The textbook used is a translation

[3] *Tarybinis Mokytojas,* October 7, 1962; December 9, 1962.

from the Russian. These advanced studies of Communist principles are designed to make the students able and purposeful fighters for atheism.[4]

To give the students further practice and competence in atheistic work, each school has a small atheist group, whose organization and guidance are the responsibility of a teacher appointed by the teachers' council. This group plans atheism days, lectures, and book discussions in the school; publishes a wall newspaper, sets up displays, makes trips to collective farms to talk atheism to the workers, and tries to develop interest and initiative in this work among the rest of the student body. Such atheist groups are especially active in boarding schools, where upper classmen are groomed as atheist-propagandists.[5]

One entertainment program, arranged by an atheist group at Kėdainiai, consisted of poetry recitations, story-telling, songs, and dramatized scenes—all slanted against priests. With jokes and mimicry, the students presented a long list of slanders and fictitious accusations. The program was staged by the school director.[6]

The Vabalninkas school group on its excursions to nearby collective farms offered a program ridiculing the Holy Scriptures. It staged various "miracles": water being converted into wine; inscriptions being made by an unseen hand; a candle lighting itself. These acts, the accompanying commentary explains, are in the same category as the miracles written about in the Old and the New Testaments and are achieved by tricks, magic, chemistry, or some other deception.[7]

To arouse greater interest in atheist activity, regional

---

[4] *Lietuvių Religinė Informacija*, January 26, 1963.

[5] *Tarybinis Mokytojas*, June 3, 1962; October 4, 1962.

[6] *Tarybinis Mokytojas*, March 10, 1963.

[7] *Tarybinis Mokytojas*, October 3, 1963.

meetings or rallies are held. On March 30, 1963, in the town of Rokiškis, a Young Atheists' rally had about 300 participants from various schools in the district. The assembly was treated to an atheist exhibit, speeches by school instructors, and a stage presentation by one of the school units.[8]

The Young Atheists of the Šilutė district schools held a similar rally in September, 1963. Their speeches and discussions were in complete agreement with their slogan, "May the atheistic idea spread!"[9]

Students are encouraged, and even forced, to join nature-study groups and there take part in atheistic projects. A group in Alytus was assigned to collect material on the theme, "Religion, the People's Opium." There are now about 700 nature-study groups in Lithuania.[10]

In 1961, church diocesan authorities were advised by the Soviet emissary for cultural affairs that all persons under 18 years of age were forbidden to attend church and especially to participate in religious services as altar boys, choristers, and aides to the priest at funerals and distribution of sacraments; nor may they march in a church procession. Those who violate this regulation, as well as the priests who permit violations, were to be severely punished.

The Communist press makes frequent assertions that anti-religious propaganda in the schools has succeeded in destroying religious propensities in the students. On June 9, 1963, Tarybinis Mokytojas ("Soviet Teacher") claimed:

Many pupils of the Joniškis district schools have long forgotten the path to the church. They now grow

[8] Lietuvių Religinė Informacija, March 31, 1963.
[9] Tarybinis Mokytojas, October 3, 1963.
[10] Lietuvos Pionierius (Vilnius), September 14, 1963.

up free of religious superstition. This is the fruit of the teachers' long and resolute effort in atheistic education. The young minds have matured through schooling and outside work. Ever louder are the militant words of the teacher, cleansing the minds of children, youth, and the workers on collective farms of the sediment remaining from the dismal past; offering love of work and life, not the bending of the knee before the altar; offering a search for human happiness not in heaven, but on earth.

Minister of Education M. Gedvilas dwelt upon the fact that school children filling out questionnaires often conceal their true convictions:

Much effort must be made that the teacher's words be sincere and clearly reflect the teacher's convictions. Otherwise our schools will be producing hypocrites. For example, in one eight-grade school in the Telšiai district, the teachers pressed their pupils to state in writing whether they believed in God. All the pupils without exception replied "No." *Even those who often go to church* gave the same answer.

Can we be pleased with such answers? That is ideological hypocrisy, which is unusually dangerous.[11]

HIGHER EDUCATION

The demands made on institutions of higher learning are equally great. Universities must train their students not only to be confirmed atheists themselves, but at the same time become propagandists for atheism. Students are given antireligious propaganda duties; if they refuse to accept them, they lose their scholarships and are expelled from school.

---

[11] *Tarybinis Mokytojas,* August 18, 1963.

Sent out to "educate" collective farm workers, they must go prepared with anti-religious lectures and answers to all possible questions. But since the rural population has a distaste for these "educators" and is inclined to stay away from lectures, the students themselves must often make up the questions and then answer their own inquiries in order to fulfill their assignment.

Even the students' summer vacations are not free of this constant atheistic grind. Lecturing and conducting discussions on anti-religious themes form an integral part of the so-called Work-and-Rest camps, where 12,000 to 14,000 students spend their summers. *Komsomol* leaders designate the locations for these camps.

KINDERGARTENS

Even children of pre-school age get a taste of anti-religious poison. At first no one suspected that the neighborhood kindergarten, where mothers must leave their children when they go to work, could also be tainted with atheism. But the instructors—"specialists" from Russia, under orders from Moscow, were soon instructing kindergarten directors how to instill the first doses of atheism into youngsters under their care. How cleverly the children are being exposed to these destructive influences may be seen from this episode described by a woman in charge of a kindergarten in the Šakiai district:

> Early in the spring my children and I planted some beans in a couple flower-pots. I told the children that the beans must be watered daily; then they would sprout and grow.
> "It is God that grows them," said one little girl named Vida.

On hearing this, the children all turned their eyes to me. I had to give a reply immediately. So I said, "Children, we shall water both of these flower-pots until the plants come up out of the ground. After they come up, we shall water and tend one plant, but the other one we will not water and will leave it for God to grow."

After a while the bean plant in the unwatered pot yellowed and dried up.

"You see, Vida, you said God can do everything. But you see, he can't even raise a bean plant without water."

All the children were then clearly convinced that they themselves grow the beans. God does not do it. There is no God.[12]

TEACHERS

The entire burden of atheistic training of the young falls on the shoulders of the teachers. Although the press is boastful at times that "every teacher is now a militant atheist capable of presenting scientific information judiciously and with convincing evidence to his pupils and to others with whom he comes in contact,"[13] and although many teachers themselves report their various successes in the anti-religious field, the teachers are frequently assailed for using insufficient effort. At a conference on adult education, Lithuanian Communist Party Secretary A. Sniečkus offered these critical comments:

> We can no longer condone the fact that some young men and women finish school without having acquired a firm, scientific outlook and sometimes even without having shaken off the load of religious superstitions.

---

[12] *Tarybinis Mokytojas,* June 16, 1963.
[13] *Tiesa,* January 6, 1962.

That is because some of the teachers do not make use of the program material provided them. In the course of inspection of atheistic teaching in the Kėdainiai district in 1961, it became obvious that some teachers were limiting themselves to a mere recital of scientific information, without drawing any conclusions that would lean toward a materialistic viewpoint and without using the teaching material for breaking down religious superstitions.[14]

Minister of Education M. Gedvilas, at an educational conference in August, 1963, spoke disapprovingly of teachers who know how to talk and use sonorous phrases, but when it comes to "standing up for the pupil and convincing his father" about atheism, they are helpless. He preferred the example set by the teachers at Stoniškiai High School, who gave notice to their families of their plan for domestically "peaceful ideological coexistence: Let the wives and children go to church, I will not go. I am an atheist! You're not going to get me!" The Minister deplored the fact that some teachers were still "enslaved by religious superstitions" and that instances of this situation had been found to exist in several schools as recently as 1962. This, he said, was absolutely incompatible with the purposes and requirements of the Soviet school, and must be dealt with drastically.[15]

In the process of molding individuals into genuine Communists, a teacher's personality must also play a part. Honorable mention is made of teachers who are "men of principle —teachers who know, when necessary, how to force a pupil or an adult not to leave a path for a bypath; teachers who, always with deep fervor, carry the Party's word, the light

---

[14] *Tiesa*, January 5, 1962.
[15] *Tarybinis Mokytojas*, August 18, 1963.

of Communist ideas, to the school children and their parents."

At the same time, complaint is lodged against the type of teacher who, "while paying lip service to the idea of communism, finds it possible in his teaching to make an adjustment between the concepts of imperialism and communism." Such a teacher "avoids giving sharp retort to those who attempt to blacken the reality of our life and to poison the pupils' consciousness with outdated remnants of the past. He is silent, and his silence becomes an implied approval of an ideology which is foreign to us."[16]

The teacher is advised to make a stronger stand against parental influence that often negates his teaching:

> Many Party committees do not sufficiently take into consideration the key point that the school is an arena of sharp ideological struggle . . . between the school and the family. An old elementary school teacher explained it this way:
>
> "School is where parental influence and school influence cross each other. The teacher, trying to inculcate in the child a materialistic philosophy, seems to be lessening the authority of the parents, while the parents, in the eyes of the child, are tearing down the authority of the teacher."
>
> At the juncture of these cross-influences, the teacher does not always take a firm, militant, ideological position. This undoubtedly impedes the entire educational effort.[17]

The difficulties involved in parent-teacher cooperation are discussed in a teachers' twice-weekly publication:

---

16 *Tarybinis Mokytojas,* August 18, 1963.
17 *Komunistas,* October, 1958.

We work, we instruct, we try to show them by argument and evidence, but when the children come home from school, what do they hear from their parents? "Listen to your teacher. Don't contradict him. But don't change your convictions. God was and ever will be. Never doubt that. It doesn't matter what the teacher tells you."[18]

Such behavior on the part of parents, says the journal, is despicable. The teachers, therefore, ought to visit the pupils' homes, organize meetings and discussions for parents, and make every effort to bring about the parents' ideological reeducation.

The article finds it scandalous that, at the very time when "the light of science has scattered the fog of stultifying religious elements, there are people among us who breathe the same air of our Communist fatherland, but who remain faithful to the religious remnants of the past"; and that parents often neglect to shape a child's views and beliefs and, instead, entangle his consciousness "in cobwebs of religious nonsense." A religious upbringing "stifles his liveliness and thirst for knowledge, promotes mental lethargy and doubt about everything around him. It rends his character."

A good book for parents, the teachers are advised, is a recent translation of *Religion's Harm to Children* by K. Bielajev, since, "with its help, it is possible to encourage parents to look soberly at their child's upbringing and to enlist the general public in active combat with antiquated religiosities."[19]

When an article in the press expressed approval of children jointly participating with their parents in the observ-

[18] *Tarybinis Mokytojas*, September 19, 1963.
[19] *Tarybinis Mokytojas*, September 15, 1963.

ance of holy days such as Christmas and Easter, since only a wicked child renounces his religious parents, and a religious person "is no criminal that one must condemn and re-nounce,"[20] contrary voices were soon heard, correcting such "erroneous" thinking. No atheist, replied a teachers' insti-tute professor, will "indulge his parents and give in to them on the question of observing religious holidays and performing religious duties." Several students added that it was wrong to take part in parents' religious festivities.[21]

PRESSURE ON PARENTS

By books, newspapers, and special bulletins, by lectures and teachers' visits to the homes, parents are increasingly pressed to accept the atheist way of thinking, both for them-selves and for their children. Even in the summer, there is no peace for parents. At Šiauliai, for instance, parents of children about to be enrolled in the first grade must them-selves attend classes, in order to learn how to aid the teachers by giving their children supplementary atheistic information at home. The parents are informed that it is the purpose of the Soviet school to train the children in such a way "that all, without exception, go out into the world as militant atheists, able to open the eyes of members of their family and of their friends and associates, who might still be believers. Atheistic militancy in a Soviet pupil is essential, so that he may have a suitable retort for those backward folk who would attempt to poison the youngster's consciousness."[22]

When conferences and individual talks with parents fail to dissuade them from their religious practices, more drastic

[20] Tiesa, October 7, 1961.
[21] Tiesa, November 29, 1961.
[22] Tarybinis Mokytojas, August 22, 1963.

measures are taken; some parents are turned over to their employment supervisors or to Party organizations, for application of more persuasive methods at their command.[23]

In some instances parents are prosecuted for "corrupting" their children with religious notions, and the children taken away from them and put under the custody of state institutions.

An Adventist preacher and his wife were charged in court with "despoiling their children's body and soul" and of depriving them of proper upbringing. The accused bravely defended himself thus: "My most important obligation (preaching) was assigned to me by God. My secondary duty—education of my children—I perform to the extent that it is consistent with the former." The court ruled that the children be taken away from this couple and entrusted to Soviet institutional care.[24]

A Panevėžys court deprived Kazimiera Juodzevičius of her maternal rights to her 13-year-old daughter and 8-year-old son for allegedly inflicting harm on them by forbidding them to attend school on Saturdays, forcing them to take part in "fanatical religious ceremonies," not giving them enough to eat, and subjecting them to physical punishment. The children also were not doing well in their studies, and it had been a year since the daughter had gone to a cinema.[25]

A court in Šiauliai took away a child from her foster mother who allegedly had taught the child prayers and forced her to lead an ascetic life.[26]

Under such conditions, few parents would have the courage of little Kristina Laugalis' father, who declared openly

---

[23] Tarybinis Mokytojas, October 6, 1963.
[24] Tiesa, May 21, 1961.
[25] Tiesa, May 29, 1962.
[26] Tarybinis Mokytojas, October 4, 1962.

at a parent-teacher meeting at Gaurė High School: "You teachers, teach religion your own way, but we parents will continue to express *our* opinion."[27]

More frequently it is a heart-rending lot that befalls parents, especially mothers, when they see their children being terrorized. At the same time, the child faces a dilemma. "My mother cries that we do not go to church," wrote one little girl to the chairman of the Atheist Council in Šiauliai. "I'm sorry for her. It's very hard for me to see her crying, and I don't know what to do."[28]

To protect children from the "harmful" influence of their parents, in 1961 the authorities began to set up boarding schools. It was planned to have enough of these schools to house 25,000 pupils by 1965. The schools, with either 8 or 11 grades, accept boys and girls from the age of seven and have a minimum of 120 pupils. An "isolation chamber" is included among the facilities. Although the regulations state that children are enrolled in boarding schools only with the consent of their parents or guardians, parental wishes are disregarded where it is found necessary to protect a child from the "harmful influence" of the home. Priority for admittance to the schools is given to orphans, children of invalids, and those whose parents cannot provide them with normal study and living conditions. This last category includes children who lack a proper atheistic environment in their home.

Boarding schools maintain strict discipline. The pupils' entire day is divided into periods for specific activities. Parents may visit their children or bring them home for a short visit only with the school director's permission. The regula-

---

27 *Tiesa*, May 5, 1963.
28 From a letter read on a Vilnius radio program, May 19, 1963.

tions allow the pupils a four-week stay at home in the summer; actually, children of religious parents do not go home
even then. For them a special "vacation" of work at a collective farm or factory is arranged.

In order to accustom boarding-school pupils to the collec-
tivist way of life, they are encouraged to participate in work
quota competitions and other Communist industrial devices.
The schools have Pioneers, *Komsomol,* and atheist organizations. These last, according to press reports, are especially
active. Upper-class pupils are being prepared as future
atheist propagandists.

Realizing the damage that is being perpetrated on the
children, many parents manage to take their children out
of school. Communists themselves admit that some schools
lose as many as 45 per cent of their pupils. They place the
number of withdrawals in one school year ending September
1, 1963, at over 10,000. Some pupils transferred to another
type of school, while others terminated their schooling without finishing eighth grade.[29]

In 1962 it was found that 64 per cent of the children
of school age in the city of Kaunas were not enrolled in any
school.[30] This may be attributed mainly to the parents' genuine fear of the irreparable moral harm that might be done to
the child in a Communist-controlled school.

To help parents understand an educational system based
on "Communist morality," a "university for parents" was
opened in Vilnius in 1960. The one-year course features
atheistic lectures, film showings, and visits to schools and
industrial concerns. Classes, attended by about 200 parents,
meet twice a month.

---

[29] *Tarybinė Mokykla,* May, 1964.
[30] *Tarybinis Mokytojas,* March 1, 1962; June 24, 1962.

VIII. THE TEACHING OF RELIGION

TEACHING OF RELIGION by priests has long been forbidden, but religious instruction by parents to their own children has been tolerated. In recent years, however, the opinion seems to be crystallizing that the parental privilege ought to be withdrawn. It is argued that the religious freedom guaranteed by the Soviet Union is intended only for adults. This viewpoint was clearly affirmed by S. P. Pavlov, first secretary of the *Komsomol* of the USSR at the Communist Youth congress in 1962. He emphasized that freedom of conscience as guaranteed by the Constitution is meant only for adults, who are answerable for their wrongdoings. No one, however, has the right to inflict spiritual harm on a child nor to exercise influence or pressure upon his still immature mind. Moreover, the teaching of religion, in Communist eyes, is nothing but religious propaganda, which the Constitution does not permit.

Article 124 of the Soviet Union Constitution clearly states: "Freedom of religious worship and freedom of antireligious propaganda is recognized for all citizens." Freedom of "religious propaganda," however, was not stipulated, and is therefore illegal. Those who take liberties in this respect are subject to prosecution.

Although the Soviet press expresses alarm that the principle of religious freedom is being grossly violated and advocates that the state take immediate steps to stop infringing upon the children's right to religious freedom, we find dedicated individuals, especially among women, who, fearless of any risk involved, round up groups of children in order to instruct them in religious doctrine. Such teachers are zealously hunted and punished for establishing clandestine church schools and for "damaging the conscience of juveniles," in violation of Soviet cult statutes. Punishment is also prescribed for the priest in whose parish such a "school" is discovered, for he is regarded as the instigator and supporter of the project.

PUNISHMENT FOR CATECHIZATION

A woman invalid, Irena Stankūnas, at the summer resort of Kulautuva and, in inclement weather, at her home in Jučioniai, taught catechism to over 30 children three times weekly and provided them with old religious booklets as reading matter. For this violation of the law, both she and the local pastor were brought to court and punished. The parents, mostly workers in a sanitarium, were accused of complicity, but when they denied any knowledge of the religious classes, the woman's guilt, according to Communist logic, was even greater, for she had operated an illegal school against the parents' wishes.

At Karmelava, a sometime seminarian, after consultation with the pastor and a group of pious women, had organized a "holy school, taught Bible stories, the mysteries of the Holy Trinity, and the lives of the saints. . . . Only when the leading organizations of the district made known their will was he forced to discontinue his pastoral work."[1] The means used to "force" him to discontinue the work was not specified in the newspaper reports.

Priests who found themselves in Siberian labor camps

---

[1] *Tarybinis Mokytojas,* September 29, 1962; May 19, 1963.

after 1955 were there usually because of their having taught catechism to children. For example, a Father Svarinskas, back from Siberia, was discovered teaching the catechism to children wherever he went, "treating them with candy and tempting them in other ways." That was reason enough to send him back to Siberia.

Another priest, Father Vytautas Balčiūnas of Salantai, was sentenced to forced labor in Siberia for "enticing children and arranging an outing for altar-boys."

In January, 1965, Father Valentinas Šikšnys, pastor at Pagramantis, drew a two-year prison sentence for giving children First Communion.[2]

On December 3, 1964, the weekly *Naujas Kelias* (The New Path), published at Marijampolė, reported that Pastor Juozas Zdebskis of Gudeliai was "deprived of his freedom" (sentenced to prison) for one year for teaching children religion and prayers.

IDEOLOGICAL TUG OF WAR

In summer-time, when the children are at home on vacation, the faithful try to undo at least some of the year's damage done at school. That considerable labor is brought to this effort is evident from the complaints voiced in the Communist press. Throughout the whole long year, it says, the teachers have labored strenuously to saturate the pupils with materialistic doctrine and to protect their minds from the muddying effect of religious truths.

But now summer arrives. . . . The teachers are vacationing. The pupils are resting. But the church

---

[2] See *Tėviškės Žiburiai* (Toronto), November 30, 1961; *Elta Press* (Rome), November, 1961; *Eltos Informacijos* (Reutlingen), February 27, 1965.

group and the pious ladies are not vacationing. It is at this very time that individuals of this category try to sway the children to their side and stuff their heads with religious superstitions. Most often it is religious little ladies, directed by priests, who organize small groups of children and teach them the "truths" of religion and how to perform religious rites. . . . Thus they tear down what the teachers have built up in a year.

At the first sign of such goings-on, teachers do everything possible "to extricate the children from the religious mire," but they reluctantly admit that "in some instances the women are successful and cram the children's heads with religious fables and Christian morality. . . . Where the teachers are not watchful, the religious crowd is sure to take over."[3]

---

[3] *Tarybinis Mokytojas,* May 19, 1963.

IX. THE PRACTICE OF RELIGION

FEAST-DAY OBSERVANCE

FOR A LONG TIME the Communists asserted that religious feast-days were only an adaptation of the old pagan feasts and as such, meaningless. The people, however, were greatly attached to them and, despite all propaganda, continued to attend church services on those days. The Communists then decided to strip the holy days of their religious character—in effect, to repaganize them—and to use them for Communist purposes. Thus Easter became "Spring Holiday"; Whitsuntide, "Shepherds' and Animals' Day." New Year's was renamed "Old Man Frost Day," and it is urged that the eve of this holiday be used for the traditional Christmas-eve supper with all its folk customs. Christmas itself is found difficult to change. Where substitutes for saints' days cannot be found, the Communists resort to holding noisy music and dance festivals directly in front of the church—usually when services are taking place inside. Similar entertainment, as well as meetings with pupils' parents, film showings, and the like, are held on Sundays to discourage church attendance.[1]

Serious efforts are being made to induce the acceptance of Communist holidays, such as: The First of May, Woman's Day, Harvest Day, Friendship of Nations Day, Cosmonaut Day, Cleanliness Day, and others.[2] The Soviet calendar, of course, recommends an October Revolution Day, a Lenin Day, a Commune of Paris Day, an International Day Against

---

[1] *Tarybinis Mokytojas,* February 22, 1962; August 26, 1962.
[2] *Literatūra ir Menas* (Vilnius), January 26, 1963.

Colonial Regimes, and special days for the press, radio, victory, physical culture, navy, air force, railroad worker, international students, artillery, tank operators, protection of children, and the Soviet Constitution. After one of these holidays the following Sunday is usually declared a work day, to make up for lost time.

CHURCH SERVICES

Church services must be omitted entirely on certain holy days or restricted to evening hours on others, depending on the whim of the local executive committee. Often only a low mass is permitted, without any choir or sermon.

Large gatherings of the faithful on feast-days are looked upon by the Communists as "provacative" religious demonstrations. The administration of the Sacrament of Confirmation used to draw such great crowds from neighboring parishes that the time and place for these ceremonies were soon regulated by the government. Later, Confirmation was made permissible only in cathedrals. Visiting priests, who were once on hand to offer assistance at special parish devotions when there were throngs of worshippers, are now forbidden to travel to other parishes without a government permit; this is obtained only with much difficulty.

OBSTRUCTIVE TACTICS

For the solemn weeklong devotions at Šiluva and Žemaičiu Kalvarija the faithful used to gather by the thousands. In recent years, pilgrims to these cherished Lithuanian shrines have been meeting with police interference. They are stopped en route for identification and questioning, under the pretext of searching for thieves and speculators; but the intent is to frighten them from completing the pilgrimage. With the added detention of priests, the devotions are becoming increasingly difficult to conduct. At the conclusion of the devotions, penal action is brought against the pastor for permitting a violation of the ordinance against public dem-onstrations.

At Žemaičių Kalvarija the Communists tore out the pictures from the Calvary chapels, but the faithful continue to visit and decorate them.

The Calvary at Vilnius has met with a sorrier state. This had been a devotional center not only for Lithuania's Catholics, but for pilgrims from Byelorussia and the Ukraine. The influx of pilgrims was especially heavy on the Feasts of the Discovery and of the Exaltation of the Holy Cross. On these feast-days in 1962 over 150,000 persons received Holy Communion. Since then, the 36 chapels—19 of them made of brick, in rococo style—dating from the 17th cen-tury, were destroyed to make way for a new Communist-planned road. Even a petition to Moscow did not prevent the destruction of this venerable site. Some pious folk still visit the place and mark the former location of a chapel with a plain little cross, but even this is forbidden.

The Stations of the Cross at Vėpriai were similarly removed, and the ground was plowed up to leave no trace of them.

On August 4, 1963, six truckloads of people from Kau-nas, Šilutė, and other places on their way to devotions at Telšiai were turned back by Communist activists stationed on various roads from early morning[3]—this, we must remem-ber, despite the constitutional guarantee of freedom of worship.

---

[3] *Komjaunimo Tiesa*, August 31, 1963.

DEBASING RELIGIOUS RITES AND CUSTOMS

Despite the intensive atheistic propaganda and anti-religious activity, the Communists have not achieved the desired results. According to their own statistics, compiled in 1962, church attendance in Lithuania had fallen off by 50 per cent, but the number of church weddings, christenings, and funerals had gone down by only 10 to 15 per cent.[4]

Especially irritating to the Communists is the knowledge that church rites are sometimes made use of by their own Party members and by the youth of the Komsomol.

The reason for this situation is attributed to the beauty, solemnity, and impressiveness of church ceremonies. Communist authorities are convinced that if civil ceremonies were made equally attractive, the people would turn away from the church. A writer in a literary journal offered the slogan "Silence the church bells!" He claims that the church maintains its influence through its holidays and its ceremonies of christening, marriage, and burial. What is needed, then, is to convert religious holidays to Soviet holidays, and church services to Soviet services.[5]

The question of Soviet marriage received special attention at a meeting of the Communist Party Central Committee in Vilnius, February 12-13, 1963. The assembly concluded that the Soviet marriage ceremony must be given solemn character and form, with music, songs, and speeches, and that it should take place in a pleasant atmosphere at a culture center and amid a large gathering of friends. The ceremony should be so impressive that the newlyweds remember the occasion all their lives. Civil ceremonies of this sort, in Communist opinion, would increase the people's interest "in the

---

[4] *Komunistas*, April, 1962.
[5] *Literatūra ir Menas*, January 26, 1963.

progressive Communist traditions and draw them away from church marriages."[6]

A special council has been established in Vilnius to search for atheistic forms of ceremony to replace religious rites related to baptisms, marriages, and funerals. It would also organize seminars for the instruction of registry office personnel in the proper performance of their ceremonial duties at these functions.[7] At the same time a committee comprised of a sculptor, a student, and a Russian director of an art gallery are working on the publication of a "ritual," with music, hymns, and all necessary components of "the new cult."[8]

NAMING THE NEW-BORN

On a date set in advance, in a beautifully decorated office of the local registrar, a baby carriage, adorned with roses, is placed on a rug. The best orchestra in the area is playing a march in honor of the godparents—name-parents, to use their term—who are prominent local Communists. The chairman and the deputies of the executive committee address the name-parents, asking them to bring up the child to be a good Communist. The name-parents then sign the registry book wherein the following pledge had been inserted:

A new person has been born. It is our collective farm's and the entire district's day of jubilation. There has come into our community still another builder of communism, a new member of the Communist community. Whatever he will be—collective farmer, doctor, engineer—our primary duty is that he grow morally

---

[6] *Lietuvių Religinė Informacija,* February 26, 1963.
[7] *Lietuvių Religinė Informacija,* October 16, 1963.
[8] *Tiesa,* October 16, 1963.

sound. . . . We accept the duty of protecting him, so that the moldy fingers of the outworn remains of the past do not touch him and the shadow of the cross does not darken his life's bright dawn. Carefully will we guard his first steps, so that he not stray from the single path that leads to communism.

A certificate is then made out with the infant's name and date of birth, set into an artistic folder, and handed to the name-parents for presentation to the child's parents. A card attached with a ribbon to the folder bears the inscription, "In remembrance of your birth." Inside is the following note:

> You are born at an unusual time, when an uncommon life—that of communism—is being established on earth. You are very much needed in the ranks of its builders, for you come to take our place and to complete that which we have begun. We believe that when you will have grown up you will justify the hopes we have placed in you, and you will be worthy of membership in the Communist community.

After this, girls in national costumes present the name-parents with flowers. Flowers are also given to the happy father for him to present to the mother. Then the entire group goes to the parents' home for entertainment, speeches, songs, etc.[9]

A quite different—somewhat circus-like—type of name-giving ceremony was witnessed in the town of Pasvalys:

> On a Saturday afternoon, Pioneers and Octobrists (Communist organizations for children) hurry to the registrar's office. . . . They quiet down and make a

---

[9] *Tiesa*, August 10, 1963.

neat line formation in the room of the festivities. . . .
The orchestra is playing a march. The name-parents
step out of an automobile. They are carrying the infant
son of Zaliauskas, who is a construction worker. Sud-
denly approaching them in measured steps, on tiptoe,
his long neck bobbing up and down, comes a stork. He
flaps his black wings, points the way and leads the
entire solemn procession indoors.

The march becomes even livelier when the stork
and the name-parents step into the decorated festivities room. The long-necked creature comes to the table,
bows before the waiting workers of the registry office,
points with his beak at the infant, and steps aside. He
has completed his assignment.

"Remigijus," is solemnly announced as the name
of little Zaliauskas.

The director of the registrar's office has scarcely
finished her speech, when the stork gives a signal and
we hear the young Pioneers. The best speakers of the
group deliver their declamations and offer their felici-
tations to little Remigijus. They wish that he follow
in their footsteps and be even better than they are. . . .
Finally they quiet down. Now several Pioneers leave
their group and . . . present a gift. It is accepted by
the name-parents, who then turn to the door. Stretched
out across their path, with the children lined up on
either side, is a Ribbon of Happiness. A Fourth-grader
hands the name-parents a pair of scissors. Let them cut
this Ribbon of Happiness and let little Remigijus begin
his life's journey accompanied by every success.[10]

In 1963 Comissar of Cult Affairs Rugienius attempted
to put church baptisms under strict control, similar to that
in Russia, where the father must submit a request to the
proper authorities and pay a high fee for a permit. Without

---

[10] *Lietuvos Pionierius,* December 28, 1963.

such a permit the priest may not baptize a child, under penalty of complete suspension from his priestly office.[11] But this system was found impractical and is not in effect in Lithuania at present.

Baptism in hospitals, however, is strictly forbidden. When it was learned that in one of Lithuania's hospitals a Catholic priest had baptized a new-born infant in danger of death, Moscow's *Izvestia* (August, 1961) gave the hospital director a severe editorial lashing for permitting this "ugly and intolerable act." What made it unpardonable was the child's recovery, which many might attribute to the powers of baptism.

The present strict control makes it almost impossible for a priest even to visit a hospital.

WEDDINGS—COMMUNIST-STYLE

Soviet civil marriages are performed every second Sunday in the district's Culture Center. An orchestra meets the arriving couples and their accompanying parties, who are dressed in national costumes. In a decorated room the newly-weds sign the marriage contract. The executive committee chairman and party officials extend their good wishes and present the young couples with flowers. To the accompaniment of a march the newlyweds descend from the platform and cut a ribbon, thus presumably opening the way to a new life. As they leave, they are greeted by friends and photographers and are showered with gifts and flowers.[12]

PARTY PROCEDURE IN BURYING THE DEAD

Atheistic burials, using red Party flags instead of church

---

[11] *Informations Catholiques Internationales* (Brussels), 1963, No. 202, p. 18.

[12] *Eltos Informacijos*, August 4, 1962.

banners and with Party chief delivering eulogies, have not caught on. Party members themselves sometimes resort to a religious burial service, thereby stirring up sharp contro-versy between the relatives of the deceased and Party officials.

One such conflict occurred with the Lionikas family in the district of Raseiniai. The son Juozas worked as secretary of the local Soviet in Balčiai. In 1961 he had been accepted as candidate to Party membership. His mother dissuaded him from joining the Party, and he remained only a candidate. When the mother died, he was told that, as a Communist, he must organize a burial befitting a Communist. Officials of the Soviet farm at Balčiai volunteered to help. They ar-ranged for three trucks to drive the coffin and the mourners to the cemetery, invited a brass band from the nearby town, ordered wreaths, gave instructions to decorate the trucks, and directed the town school teachers to participate in the funeral with their pupils. The funeral procession was to be very solemn and *without a priest*—the first Communist fu-neral in that area. Hence it must be most impressive.

But the relatives of Mrs. Lionikas reasoned differently: since the deceased had been a deeply devout Catholic, she should have a Catholic burial. Beside her coffin they placed a crucifix and lighted candles, and the wake was one con-tinuous round of hymns and prayers. The Communists were enraged at the sight. Unable to persuade the family to aban-don this old-fashioned ritual, they called off the band, took back the wreaths, and ordered the truck drivers to go back with their vehicles. Meanwhile the crowd of mourners took the body of the deceased woman to the church for a requiem service and then, with the priest, to the cemetery.

Following this event the press excoriated the Party organizations for their inept handling of atheistic activities.[13]

Those who bury their loved ones with religious services may expect to experience certain unpleasantries, such as reduction or temporary suspension of pay, or even dismissal from work. They also get a public namecalling in the press as reactionaries, retrogrades, and obstructionists to the advancement of communism.

A high school principal at Skapiškis, attending his mother's funeral, was understandably careful to remain outside when the coffin was taken into church. He was seen, however, following the coffin to the cemetery, where a priest blessed the burial ground. Questioned, the teacher defended himself by blaming his outoftown relatives for the funeral arrangements. Nevertheless, he was found guilty of permitting the recitation of the rosary by the deceased woman's friends gathered around the coffin, and he lost his school position.[14]

During the years of Lithuania's independence it was the custom on the eve of All Souls' Day to visit the graves of the dead and to decorate them with flowers and candles. Religious services were held in the cemeteries, and sermons were preached for the faithful assembled. The graves of national heroes were especially honored. Now, under the Communists, some of the cemeteries have been abolished, while the remaining ones have seen monuments destroyed, and graves, especially those of the soldiers, barbarously desecrated. Since this has not deterred the faithful from showing their Christian respect for the dead, the Communists have now begun to honor their own heroes. In the cemetery at

---

[13] *Tiesa*, February 1, 1963.
[14] *Komjaunimo Tiesa*, November 21, 1962.

Panevėžys, for instance, Communist dead were extolled with speeches, reading of poetry, including a poem called "Requiem," and playing of Wagner's "Funeral March." It is planned to make these memorial programs annual affairs.[15]

CLOSING OF CHURCHES

To the Communists, churches, as centers of religious life, are an abomination which must be done away with, under one pretext or another. The closing of churches has been going on since the beginning of the Soviet occupation of Lithuania. Even the new church in Klaipėda, for whose construction a government permit had been issued during the brief period of relaxation, cannot be used for religious purposes. When it was completed in 1960, the Communists brought charges against its pastor, Father Liudas Povilonis, and his assistant, Father Bronius Burneikis, for alleged misappropriation of funds, illegal use of building materials, and speculation in foreign exchange. After an 11-day public trial, the pastor was sentenced to eight years in prison and the assistant to four years. Five who had been in charge of building materials were also sentenced. The church steeple has been torn down, and the church itself converted by the Communists into a concert hall.

Churches were closed recently in Mažeikiai, Old Žagarė, Kėdainiai, and Pašilė. A total of 448 churches and chapels in Lithuania have been closed. Still remaining open are 574 churches. But Soviet laws provide for numerous situations when the churches may be disposed of, as, for instance: when they are unable to meet their tax assessments, when they lose their congregation, when there is no priest avail-

---

[15] *Literatūra ir Menas,* April 6, 1963.

able, when the site is needed for residential construction, when the building is old, etc.

Vilnius, Lithuania's ancient capital and site of numerous artistic and monumental churches, has been severely af' fected by the closing of many of its important shrines. The famous St. Stanislaus Basilica, originally built by King Jo' gaila in 1387, rebuilt in 1419 by Lithuania's Grand Duke Vytautas, and again rebuilt in 1530, 1610, and 1655, has been turned into an art gallery. Twenty-five other Vilnius churches,[16] most of them centuries old, have been appro'

[16] a) The Church of St. John the Baptist and St. John the Apostle, erected in 1387 by King Jogaila and Grand Duke Vytautas, is now a depot for paper supplies. b) Church of All Saints, erected in 1620, is a warehouse. c) St. Francis Church (Bernardine), erected in 1492 by King Casimir Jogailaitis, destroyed during the Russian invasion in 1655, and rebuilt by Lithuania's Grand Hetman Pacas, has been converted to an art institute. d) Church of the Apostles Phillip and Jacob, erected in 1642, rebuilt by the Dominicans in 1690-1727, is closed, abandoned. e) Church of the Sacred Heart of Jesus, erected in 1913, is used as a library. f) Church of Mary the Comforter, erected in 1746-68, now serves various Communist needs. g) St. Ignatius Loyola Church (Jesuit, later Marian), erected in 1622, contains a motion picture studio and living quarters. h) St. George Church (Seminary), erected by Prince Radvila in 1506, has been made into a library. i) St. Bartholomew Church, erected in 1664, is a warehouse. j) St. Joseph Church, erected by Prince Radvila and Bishop Kasakauskis in 1798, has been adapted to secular use. k) Church of the Holy Trinity (Basilian), erected in the 16th century, is a storage place used by the city philharmonic orchestra. l) Church of the Redeemer (Trinitarian), erected in 1694, is a library. m) Church of Jesus Crucified, erected in the 17th century, is a warehouse. n) Church of the Holy Trinity, erected in 1832, is reserved for Communist needs. o) Church of St. Casimir, the Patron Saint of Lithuania (Jesuit), erected by Cardinal Carlos Ferdinand Vaza, King Sigismundus III and Lithuania's Grand Chancellor Leonas Sapiega to commemorate St. Casimir's canonization in 1604, has been made into a museum of atheism. p) Church of the Ascension (Missionary), erected in 1698, is converted into a warehouse. q) Church of Divine Providence, erected in 1913, is a warehouse. r) Church of the Assumption (Franciscan), erected in the 14th century, is a warehouse. s) Church of Mary the Victorious (Redemptorist), is used for offices. t) Holy Cross Church, erected in 1336, is a warehouse. u) St. Stephen the Martyr Church, erected in 1600, is a warehouse. v) St. Catherine Church (Benedictine), erected in 1622, is a warehouse. w) Church of the Sacred Heart of Jesus and St. Francis de Sales (Visitandine), erected in 1694, is used for a club. x) Church of St. Michael the Archangel (Bernardine), erected in 1594 by Lithuania's Grand

riated by the Communists for various profane purposes. Of the churches known to have existed in Vilnius in 1939[17] only twelve are still open.

The city of Kaunas in 1940 had 17 churches and 13 chapels. It now has 9 churches and not one chapel.[18]

Churches that have not been closed are, of course, government property. The faithful are permitted to use them upon payment of very high assessments, which have been steadily increasing. Since churches are classified as places of amusement and are taxed according to the size of the plot of land they occupy, their taxes have amounted to between 1,000 and 5,000 rubles per annum.

Some of Lithuania's churches have great artistic merit and constitute the finest examples of architectural monuments in the country. Many, though closed for worship, were taken over by the state in recognition of their significance to the Soviet Union. Some that had suffered damage during

---

Chancellor, Hetman Leonas Sapiega, seriously damaged by the Cossacks in 1665, rebuilt in baroque style in 1762, has been turned into an exhibition hall and warehouse for home furnishings. y) Church of the Sweetest Heart of Mary (The Family of Mary Sisters), is converted to an apartment house.

[17] As listed in *Catalogus Ecclesiarum et Cleri Archidioecesis Vilnensis Pro Anno Domini* 1939 (Vilnius).

[18] a) Church of the Holy Trinity, erected in 1634 for the Bernardine Sisters and later made into a parish church, during the second Soviet occupation was used by the seminary for worship and classes. It is now made into a dance hall. b) St. George Church (Seminary), erected in 1471 for the Bernardine order of monks and assigned in 1864 to the Kaunas Seminary, is now used for storage space. c) St. Francis Xavier Church (Jesuit), erected in 1720, baroque style, is a warehouse. d) St. Nicholas Church (Benedictine), erected in the 15th century, is appropriated for secular use. e) Church of the Holy Sacrament (Student), erected in the 17th century by the Dominicans, has been made into a warehouse. f) St. Gertrude Church (Marian), one of the oldest churches in Kaunas, is now a paper warehouse. g) Church of the Resurrection, built before World War II as a national memorial with donations from all over Lithuania, has been appropriated by the Communists for a television factory. h) St. Michael Church (Military), of Byzantine architecture, erected in 1891-95, is converted to a museum. i) Church of the Exaltation of the Holy Cross was razed by the Communists in 1950.

the war were restored. However, when Soviet Premier Khrushchev at the Communist Party Central Committee meeting in January, 1961, in Moscow, expressed his opposition to preservation of monuments and the waste of funds for their repair, the Party line with respect to safeguarding monuments was also rapidly changed in Lithuania. It was soon discovered that inspectors of architectural monuments "had violated the Marxist-Leninist principles as they affect the cultural heritage and had idealized feudal antiquities."[19]

[19] *Tiesa*, July 27, 1961.

X. THE CASE AGAINST THE CLERGY

THE COMMUNIST PRESS frequently stresses the idea that a distinction must be made between an ordinary lay religious person and a member of the clergy. The former need not be condemned; instead, he requires methodical instruction. It is the latter category of individuals, those willful pur-veyors of religion, that must be engaged in a hard struggle.[1]

It is the priests, in the eyes of the Communist Party, who are the incorrigible reactionaries and deadly enemies of the Soviet order. It is the priests who bear the greatest respon-sibility for the failure of the atheistic propaganda apparatus to achieve its desired objectives. There can be no relations with them except as adversaries.

"PRIESTS VIOLATE FREEDOM OF CONSCIENCE"

Although legally "servants of the cults may preach ser-mons of religious nature, the law strictly forbids anyone from using religious gatherings for political declarations con-trary to the interests of the Soviet states, for encouraging the faithful to renounce their civic obligations, and for inducing them to withhold their active participation in Socialist public life."[2]

How does the clergy violate these laws? The Commu-nists list the following offenses:

---

[1] *Tiesa*, October 7, 1961.
[2] A. Veščikovas, *Tarybiniai Įstatymai apie Religinius Kultus* (Vilnius, 1963), pp. 22-23.

Priests refuse to recognize the new ethics and morality that are flourishing in Lithuania. From the pulpit they whine about the decline of virtue, and they unashamedly slander and threaten. Seeing that the youth are moving away from the church, they concentrate their strongest appeals on young girls, while the mothers are given stories of frightening scenes that transpire in the life of a loose-living daughter after she forsakes God. Thus they openly denounce Soviet society. The clergy is especially solicitous of the younger generation. Often without even consulting the parents, they employ every means at their disposal to instruct the children in catechism and urge the mothers to continue such instruction at home. Many priests make every effort to remove the children from Soviet educational institutions, though this is a terrible deprivation to inflict upon a child's future.[3]

Specific instances are cited in the press of priests preaching falsehoods "against Communist truth." In the cemetery of Alizava, for example, on March 25, 1963, at the interment of the body of Vytautas Dešrys, student at the Academy of Agriculture, Pastor Jonas Jatulis disclosed in a sermon that the deceased, though a member of the Communist Youth organization, was actually a practicing Catholic. This statement about the dead youth, who "had been an atheist" and even wrote verses against "the cassocked ravens," the Communists labelled outright slander. Using this opportunity, they uncovered the pastor's earlier "crimes": his concealment in a church of several partisans and his ties with the partisan leader and "murderer" Starkus. For this he had served a prison term in Siberia, but after the prison experience he showed no improvement. . . .[4]

---

[3] Svyturys (Vilnius), January 30, 1961.
[4] Tiesa, April 28, 1963.

Communists cannot abide sermons on the nobility and holiness of faith as preached by Pastor Kurmauskas, if this same priest commits such transgressions as baptizing a child without the mother's consent, or speaking at the burial of a woman and daughter and pleading for mercy for the killer —their demented husband and father—by saying: "Remem' ber forever the compassion of our heavenly Father. Let us not judge anyone here on earth. The Lord God is the judge of all of us. . . ." Such preaching is "boundless hypocrisy."

There was one priest who gave sermons that disparaged Soviet schools. Another priest had reproached the collec' tive farm workers for not going to church in the busy summer season. Priests are accused of speaking out against science, atheism, and Soviet organizations; of reacting wrongly to the methods employed to strengthen atheistic propaganda; of distorting this propaganda as an attack on religion and the church, thus stirring up the faithful against the Com' munists.[5] "These servants of God who preach the moving sermons, who speak of the love of one's neighbor, and who explain God's commandments, are refined hypocrites preying upon the feelings of the faithful."[6]

A sermon on even the most innocent religious topic is offensive to the Communists, for they regard sermons as an aid to the spread and perpetuation of superstitions which communism strives to eradicate. Sermons are an expression of resistance to Communist ideology. As such, they are the target of the most scathing epithets.

"PRIESTS CULTIVATE NATIONALISM"

Here are several examples of nationalistic "crimes" as reported in the Communist press:

---

[5] Veščikovas, op. cit., pp. 5-6.
[6] Tarybinis Mokytojas, June 21, 1959.

"To implant nationalism in the younger generation, some priests have conceived the idea of using national costumes in religious ceremonies. The pastor at Šiluva has already acquired twelve national costumes and the pastor at Molėtai, twenty."[7]

Father Juozas Stasiulis has begun to discharge "nationalistic fumes" in verse form, "worshipping nationalist bandits and Hitler's occupying forces, and heaping scorn and slander on the working classes."[8]

Since World War II the clergy is said to be supporting nationalists, who are averse to any friendship with the Russians.

"PRIESTS VIOLATE SOVIET CULT REGULATIONS"

The clergy is charged with interference with Communist construction projects and alienation of the young from Communist educational institutions. A Communist Youth organ[9] reported that a school director was renovating the school, while his pupils were renovating the church. It happened at Žigaičiai. By taking the pupils on his motorcycle to the beach and plying them with candy and other favors, the pastor was said to have gained the youngsters' confidence and then to have used them for his own purposes: they cleaned the church paintings, and he taught them prayers and how to serve at mass. He even organized a group to do repair work on the church. "The school, however, remains unrenovated." Such tactics of the priest are regarded as a deliberate attempt to obstruct the school's educational program.

---

[7] Veščikovas, op. cit., p. 4.

[8] Tiesa, January 14, 1962.

[9] Komjaunimo Tiesa, August 8, 1959.

Priests are held guilty of interfering with the freedom of conscience of children. They fail to condemn the parents, who force their children to attend church, punish them when they neglect to learn their prayers, or are lax in performing religious rites. Instead, the priests censure parents whose children do not come to church. "The Soviet laws do not forbid priests to urge parents to teach their children religious matters, but the laws do not permit the use of compulsion on children who do not wish to study religion. Such actions by the priests cannot be tolerated. Parents must understand that the child is not only their child and a member of their family, but a member of the Soviet collective, a son of his Socialist Fatherland."[10]

Thus priests are held responsible even for what happens in the home.

LIMITATIONS IMPOSED ON PASTORAL WORK

To prevent churchmen from encroaching on the citizens' freedom of conscience, Soviet laws on religious cults forbid religious ceremonies outside the house of worship without a special permit. It is forbidden for servants of a cult to visit the homes of their faithful and perform therein devotions and religious rites. Such visitations constrict the Soviet citizens' freedom.[11]

In practical terms, a priest may not baptize a child or administer the sacraments to a dying person at home or in a hospital. This is the case even though, officially, "religious services outside the church and other houses of prayer may be performed only upon request of the dying or gravely ill."[12]

---

[10] Veščikovas, op. cit., p. 6.
[11] Ibid., p. 24.
[12] Ibid., p. 25.

A letter from Lithuania describes actual cases:

> E. A. was a patient in the city hospital a whole month. He asked for a priest, but no one called him. Instead, the watch became even more strict lest a priest come there secretly. In a hospital, though one begs and pleads for a priest, it doesn't help a bit. Recently an acquaintance of ours died. . . . She begged for a priest before she died, but it was of no use.[13]

PRIESTLY CHARITY IS UNLAWFUL

A priest may not give aid to needy parishioners in illness or distress. If he does so, he violates the law. The Communists boast:

> There is no need for church alms. Poverty, hunger, unemployment have been liquidated in our country. . . . Our citizens are guaranteed full care in sickness, unemployment and old age, but churchmen seize upon distribution of alms to maintain their influence among the faithful. With their charitableness they hope to strengthen religion's authority and ensnare new victims in its traps. Soviet laws deal a blow to these hypocritical church acts.[14]

KEEPING RECORDS IS UNLAWFUL

> The function of the clergy is to perform religious rites only. . . . Catholic priests, in violation of Soviet laws, attempt to take over the entire control of the parish and to use it for their own selfish purposes. . . . They exploit their role of leadership to strengthen religion and the church.[15]

---

[13] *Elta Press*, November, 1963.
[14] Veščikovas, *op. cit.*, pp. 25-26.
[15] *Ibid.*, pp. 7, 34.

A pastor, therefore, can do no administrative work, such as taking a census of his parishioners, keeping a record of the sacraments received by them, or issuing birth certificates or other documents. He cannot ask for or accept any fee for his church-related services. Any of these acts constitute violations of the law.

OUTSIDE ASSOCIATIONS ARE UNLAWFUL

Since a priest is now limited to performing religious rites, he may not associate with people outside his church; his influence can only be harmful. He has no rights, only duties: to pay taxes, to submit to government regulations and carry out its orders, and on election day to vote for Communist candidates. In effect, he is removed from public life.

When a pastor in Akmenė was seen attending a performance of a play by visiting artists of the Vilnius State Theatre and seated in the very front row with distinguished Communists, a sharp protest was made by the acting company's Party agent. How dare they seat in such an honorable location one who has no status in progressive Communist society! The agent upbraided the organizers of the play and the local Party group for issuing an invitation to so unworthy a creature.[16]

The Communists cannot tolerate the clergy's attempts to seek contact with the people. It is noted that "some priests try to organize young people's choirs, excursions . . . and hold special devotions for the youth, give special sermons to the young."[17] Even Moscow's journal *Ogoniok* (1960, No. 39) reported one priest in Lithuania who organized a sports club, another who arranged an evening of dancing,

---

16 *Tiesa*, July 9, 1963.
17 Veščikovas, *op. cit.*, p. 6.

a third who formed book-reading circles—all names and locations carefully noted and all projects having greater success
than similar party-planned activities.

During the summer of 1960, a Vilnius Polish Communist newspaper, *Czerwony Sztandar,* was writing reproach-
fully about Father Vladas Novickis, who was making the
rounds of his parishioners by auto to propagate "religious
superstitions."

The Communists are also annoyed over Father A. Kani-
šauskas' "hypocrisy:" acting like a great proletarian, he goes
to work with the people, fixes their clocks, stoves, and
kitchen utensils, offers medical aid to the sick, and even has
ready remedies for ailing livestock.[18] The press demands that
all such hypocritical actions, which are merely coercion of
people's conscience, be stopped. The Commissar for Cult
Affairs is, of course, quite ready to oblige by cancelling the
priest's work permit or by calling for his removal to another,
more isolated place and, especially, away from the youth.

"PRIESTS DESTROY PUBLIC PROPERTY"

Since all cemeteries have been taken over by the state,
the pastor and the parish have no jurisdiction over them.
This is why one pastor was accused of cutting down trees
in his parish burial grounds for his own use.[19] Another was
fined 300 rubles and sentenced to six months in prison for
cutting down trees, which, "on falling to the ground,
crushed some graves and toppled over crosses"—such was
the judge's given motivation for the sentence.[20]

Not infrequently, cemetery crosses and other religious

---

[18] *Sluota* (Vilnius), January, 1963.
[19] *Tiesa,* June 13, 1959.
[20] *Tiesa,* January 6, 1962.

symbols are overturned by *Komsomol* members in the course
of night raids, and civil authorities have begun to frown
upon the erection of tombstones of religious character.

PRIESTS "COERCE" THE FAITHFUL TO MAKE
DONATIONS

According to Soviet laws, all contributions for church
maintenance and support of the clergy must be voluntary.
Yet still another accusation against priests maintains:

> Many cult servants force the faithful to meet fixed as-
> sessments, thus making church donations compulsory.
> . . . Not infrequently this money is then filched and
> squandered on feasts, new houses, automobiles, and
> other luxuries. It is the duty of civic organizations to
> protect the faithful from the greediness of these preda-
> tory characters. The submitted material on this question
> is being duly investigated by organs of the court and
> the prosecuting agency."[21]
> Soviet laws forbid compulsory assessments for the
> benefit of religious communities, the bishop's curia, theo-
> logical seminaries, or anything else. For the needs of
> religious communities only voluntary contributions may
> be collected. The collections are to be made in the house
> of prayer and by the faithful themselves, not by the
> priests. The funds must be administered by the religious
> communities, not by the priests."[22]

Specifically, it is charged against the clergy that, "basing
their action on Church canon laws, often for selfish reasons,
they extract compulsory payments for maintenance of religious associations." Under the priests' direction, a church

---

21 Veščikovas, *op. cit.*, pp. 34-35.
22 *Ibid.*, pp. 6-7.

committee goes from house to house, setting the precise amount each family must donate. For example: Pastor Petras Galkys of Gudanava had instructed his collectors to collect five rubles from each family as payment for 1963; Pastor Gražys of Sudeikiai had sent out written statements demanding an annual church donation of 30 to 50 rubles.[23] Communist critics of the clergy say that even blackmail is used.

"PRIESTS PILFER PARISH FUNDS"

Communists say that money belonging to religious communities is spent by priests for drinking bouts, which, at least for Pastors Laimutis Blynas and Kazys Girnius, are annual affairs. This, too, is against the law. What the Communists are referring to is the usual dinner and reception given to the visiting clergy on the occasion of the annual parish feastday (when such observance was still permitted).

In the interval when the persecution of the church was slightly relaxed, quite a few wardamaged churches were renovated, repaired, and made usable again. This required fundraising. If the churches had been left in disrepair, there was always the danger of losing them. But the Communists were quick to accuse the clergy of reaping personal profit from these repair projects. Here are just three examples from among many:

A pastor and his successor at Antalieptė assessed their parishioners for the necessary church repairs; for the money collected, one built himself a house, and the other bought himself a motorcycle.[24] A priest at Viekšniai made a personal housetohouse collection and then bought two houses in

23 *Ibid.*, p. 7.
24 *Tiesa,* June 13, 1959.

Mažeikiai.[25] A pastor in Adomynė used his collection to get himself a motorcycle and a car and to build a home for his brother-in-law, the sacristan.[26]

The Communist press publishes numerous charges of this nature. What it fails to mention, however, is that purchases of houses is directly related to the earlier confiscation of parish rectories, which left the priests without shelter. Since a parish has no juridical right to own property, title to a house had to be assumed by an individual—in this case, the pastor. Where a new house was built, it was done so with the government's permission. Yet the pastor was later accused of using church money for its building.

Several of the newly-built parish houses were confiscated because the priest had no proof that he built it with his own personal funds—funds which a priest is not legally permitted to possess in the first place. Obviously, they say, the priest has unlawfully appropriated money belonging to the parish. And so on *ad infinitum*. The purpose of these accusations and malignments is to stir up dissension between the parishioners and their priests.

PASTORAL VISITATIONS ARE BANNED

The annual visitation of parishioners was often a priest's sole personal contact with his people. Traditionally, this was an opportunity for each family to contribute something for the priest's material support. To discourage this contact, the Communists forbade the use of wagons for bringing back the donated grain and other farm products. Later they made his cash gifts taxable. Finally, in 1961, the council of ministers of Soviet-occupied Lithuania stopped these visitations

---

25 *Tiesa*, January 14, 1962.
26 *Tiesa*, March 19, 1960.

entirely, explaining that the annual trips had become only "a means of plundering the faithful . . . and that the rough behavior of the cult servants and the irritating questioning to which the populace were forced to submit had become very unpopular."[27]

With so many restrictions, it is understandable why a priest in Lithuania, in the course of attending to his pastoral duties, is bound to come into conflict with "Soviet laws pertaining to religious cults" and to be subject to prosecution for violation of one or another of the numerous regulations with which the religious are shackled.

COMMUNISTS APPRAISE THE "NEW" CHURCH

The clergy have become more dangerous to the Communist regime because they have "modernized"—have adopted new techniques and are exploring new themes in their sermons. The church is seen as able to accommodate itself to the latest scientific advances and to adapt its dogmas and cult practices to existing social-political situations.

In a critical analysis of the more common "forms of religious ideologies" in the Soviet Union, Mcedlov, a prominent Soviet journalist, states that Catholic priests in the Soviet Union—meaning, in this instance, Lithuania—no longer call collective farms "instruments of the devil," but advocate working there "decently and conscientiously," even in their sermons. Also, in contrast to earlier denunciations of Pioneers and *Komsomol,* the priests advise parents to enroll their children in these organizations, adding only the admonition that they "not forget the church." The Church rep-

---

[27] Veščikovas, *op. cit.,* p. 4.

resents itself as the sole moral bulwark and depicts "the godless" in the worst possible light. Yet once in a while it holds devotions for the conversion of "erring atheists."

In the same critical treatise, the author sees the Church as trying to preserve the nationalistic spirit. This is especially noticeable in Lithuania, Latvia, and Byelorussia. The village clergy remain traditionalists, still clinging to the cult of "the miraculous and holy places." In a published proclamation, they speak of "the First of May as the Feast of St. Joseph the Carpenter, and urge the people to emulate him." When they offer a word of sympathy or material aid to a lonely mother, a widow, or the sick, it is done, says this critic, only to bind these persons to the ideology and the institution of the church. With their "religious favors" in hand they intrude into private homes at christenings, funerals and the like. What is most interesting, they have been known to organize the purchase of entire stocks of atheistic books.

Mcedlov then speaks about the changing church practices, pointing to the increase in the number of Masses, which may now be held in the evening, and the liberalization of the rules of fasting. He notes that church feast-days are frequently transferred to state holidays or days of rest, and that priests go to great lengths to decorate their churches, assembling numerous paintings and sculptures. They make equally earnest efforts to raise the level of church music and singing. Even village churches sometimes have city choirs and music ensembles participating in their services. The latest technical advances—microphones, loud speakers, tape-recorders—are put to use. That "religious belief and relations with the church organization still exist in certain segments of society" is attributed to the weakness of the atheist-Communist propaganda campaign.[28]

In other words, the Communists acknowledge that the clergy "have adapted themselves to the new conditions" and can no longer be accused of backwardness, ignorance, or reactionism. Making general assertions that the church supports imperialism, bourgeois nationalism, and fascism has no effect on the faithful, who respect and uphold the clergy. Also, continuous charges that priests "violate Soviet laws" make no impression on the faithful, who are themselves guilty of similar "violations." The Communists are therefore urged to employ new tactics: destroy the priests' authority by exposing their "two-facedness," "amorality," and "greediness."

Instructions for use of the new tactics have been issued "from higher up." At the July, 1959, conference of atheist lecturers in Vilnius, the conclusion was that speakers must appeal not only to the listener's mind but also to his feelings. It was reasoned that "the faithful are scandalized when their priests' behavior does not conform with their sermons. It is necessary, therefore, to continue speaking and writing about the priests' recent assistance to Hitlerites and bourgeois nationalists and to uncover the clergy's true character and amorality. Militant atheistic propaganda based on documented material cannot be called offensive to the feelings of the faithful. It is important that our militant word inspire those who are still bound to religious superstition to reason soberly and to believe in a bright future."

Soon after these instructions were made public, newspapers were filled with accusations against individual priests

---

[28] M. Krupavičius, "Katalikybės Taktika ir Ideologija Sovietų Sajungoje," *Draugas* (Chicago, September 8, 1962).

who had reportedly aided the German fascists, cooperated with Lithuania's partisan fighters, participated in the exe cution of innocent people, and the like. Based on "archive documents," "voluntary confessions," "minutes" of diocesan conferences, "diaries," and other "evidence," the clergy's wartime activity was written up in great detail. It was brought out that the religious of Lithuania had sided with "bourgeois nationalists" and bitterly fought against "the people's government." This is the type of material found in the book *Twentieth Century Inquisitors* by E. Žemaitis, published in 1961. Among other anti religious books intent on "unmasking" the priests are: *Nationalist Activity of Lithuanian Clericals, The Image of the Clergy, Spreaders of Ignorance, The Two Faced,* and *How Priests Deceive the Working People.*

Periodical publications, too, are full of Communist con cocted stories of how this or that priest before the war had extorted huge fees for rendering this or that religious favor; how priests refused their services to the gravely ill if the possessions of the dying were not bequeathed to the church or the pastor; how they assisted in the wartime mass murder of innocent people. They publish tales of their immoral acts with their maidservants, their organization and support of the partisans, and their misuse of church funds. There is no offense against morality, humanity, and existing laws of which the clergy is not accused. Places are named where the accused may never have visited. "Facts" are given in evi dence, though such facts never took place and the persons mentioned never existed. Bishops' conferences are described as drunken revelries, at which the bishops addressed one an other as "Mister" and discussed how to hand over Lithuania to Hitler and how to thank him for the murders committed.

Religious orders are not spared their share of calumny, each order covered in a separate publication designed to "prove" that all of them—Jesuits, Franciscans, Marians—have been spying centers for the Vatican from the very beginning.

This constant defamation of the clergy is done not only in print; it is the main theme of atheist meetings and lectures. For example, the atheist council committee in Šiauliai arranges a lecture every Thursday to delve into the work of the clergy. At one of these lectures, wrote *Tiesa* (January 6, 1962), the "unmasking" of several priests made a deep impression on the faithful when they were shown that the Canon of Sts. Peter and Paul Church was a "fierce nationalist and an ally of bandits" (the usual appelation for members of the underground resistance forces).

At Gruzdžiai House of Culture, before a gathering of 600 collective farm workers, Father E. Semaška was "unmasked" as a former organizer of partisan fighters and a friend of Uselis, a partisan who was caught and executed.[29] This priest had already served a term in Siberia, but the Communists have not stopped molesting him.

Because of an article in the Communist journal *Švyturys* in 1962, which initiated violent agitation against the "antisocial and amoral activity" of Father J. Žvinys, pastor at Širvintai, letters were sent to the executive committee, meetings were called, and resolutions were passed, demanding that the priest be brought to justice. His "crimes" were his alleged organization of *Šauliai* (Lithuanian national guard) units, his forbidding that the people pray in their native tongue, and his persecution of national minorities.[30] This

[29] *Tiesa*, June 11, 1963.
[30] *Tiesa*, October 27, 1962, and *Svyturys*, September 30, 1962.

organized pressure against Father Žvinys led to his "dereg' istration" by the Cult Commissar; i.e., he was forbidden to perform priestly duties and forced to move out of the city.

To what degree of absurdity the Communists carry their charges of crime and misdemeanor against priests may be judged from an incident described in *Tiesa* (February 25, 1962): A prayer-book was allegedly found in the pocket of a man who had killed his wife and infant daughter. This was presented as evidence that the murderer was a believer and knew his pastor. Moreover, the unfortunate victims were buried with religious services. All this was taken as proof that the man had been driven to murder by religious fanaticism instilled by the priests. The church was thus made an accomplice of the murderer. Quite frequently, if the accused admits before a court that he is religious, the church is made a co-defendant.

Speculation is a frequent charge against the clergy. Since there is a great shortage of devotional objects—rosaries, crosses, medals, pictures, and since they cannot be imported from abroad, old pictures are photographed and duplicated and rosaries are made of cherry pits. When priests are dis' covered to have connections with this illegal activity, they are punished for speculation—carrying on a business for personal gain.

A Jesuit priest, after returning from Siberia, where he had served a seven-year term at hard labor for "forming a secret anti-Soviet organization" in Šiauliai, could not forget the shortage of devotional articles in Siberia. For the mass stipends that came to him from Siberia he would send his correspondents crosses, medals, and rosaries. When these transactions were discovered, he was sentenced to seven years in prison and was again deported to Siberia.[31] The recipients of the devotional objects were also punished.

THE FAMILY AS A WEAPON

Even a priest's relatives are used against him. A priest's mother, for instance, is compelled to write an open letter to a newspaper, renouncing her son. (One such mother is known to have gone insane and died after the publication of her letter.)

Vilnius Radio, on April 13, 1962, broadcast an open letter from Kazimieras Budraitis to his brother priest, accus' ing the clergy of a parasitic existence and of allying them' selves with the enemies of the Lithuanian people while lay persons like himself were making a living from honest toil. The letter urged the priest to "make amends for his useless work by transferring to some other occupation."

A letter addressed to a brother priest in Kaunas appeared in *Tiesa* on January 14, 1962. It seems that when the parents died and little Vladas (now the writer of the letter) was put in an orphanage, the brother priest had him removed and brought to his own home, then sent him to school and looked after him. Now that Vladas was able to stand on his own feet, the Communists used him to repay his brother with their brand of gratitude. On finding in the priest's li' brary "volumes denouncing the Soviet order," Vladas left his brother and, determined never to return, wrote to him as follows:

> We must go our separate ways. My path is that of conscientious work, of resolute study with Soviet youth. . . . I am now a member of a large group in a

---

[31] *Svyturys*, March 15, 1963 and *Elta Press*, June, 1963.

certain enterprise and am continuing my studies. I am happy not only because I escaped your religious effluvia, the trap of Jesuitism, but, more important, I feel I am a free and useful member of society. . . . It was my conscience and not revenge or hatred of you that dictated this letter. If you were only my brother and not a priest, not a preacher of religion, perhaps I wouldn't be writing this, but every day you inflict moral damage on hundreds of others exactly as you damaged my mental faculties. I do not want other such victims falling into your snare.[32]

Priests who have returned from Siberia in ill health but unbroken in faith and apostolic spirit are especially singled out for the "unmasking" treatment. The faithful have deep respect for them, take care of them, and treat them as martyrs. To diminish their influence, the Communists try in every way to blacken their names, heaping every kind of calumny upon them. A book whose object is to besmirch the clergy, titled *Murderers in the Embrace of the Church*, marshals an array of what is intended to be incriminating evidence against a long list of clergymen.[33]

The offenses of these churchmen, purportedly corroborated by proper witnesses, were: giving aid to the "nationalist bandits" (partisans), shooting innocent people during the Nazi occupation, and acting against the People's government. The "self-incriminating evidence" plus their "confessions" brought them and many others severe sentences and exile to Siberia.

[32] *Tiesa,* May 26, 1959.
[33] Bishops Borisevičius and Ramanauskas; priests: L. Šapoka, P. Janušaitis, A. Viskantas, P. Lygnugaris, Msgr. J. Laukaitis, Ed. Vaišnoras, A. Juška, J. Normanas, A. Kiela, Pr. Gustaitis, J. Lankauskas, P. Jasas, St. Rudžionis, J. Puzonas, A. Ažubalis, E. Semaška, Z. Neciunskas, Pr. Šliumpa, A. Ylius, G. Dunda, J. Juodaitis, J. Urbanavičius.

Lithuanian priests returned from Siberian prisons to Lithuania.

The same group in clerical garb.

Bishop Teofilius Matulionis

Bishop Teofilius
Matulionis
in a
Siberian
prison camp.

Bishop Pranas Ramanauskas. Left, as auxiliary bishop of Telšiai diocese about 1946; below, as he appeared upon his return from exile in Siberia ten years later.

Archbishop Mečislovas Reinys.
Parished while prisoner in 1953
at Vladimir, Siberia.

Bishop Vincentas Borisevičius,
condemned to death in 1946.

Prayer-book, hand-written and bound by Lithuanian girls in Siberian prison.

Professor Pranas Dovydaitis, a distinguished Catholic leader, deported to Siberia June 15, 1941.

Lithuanian graves in Siberia.

Bishop Julius Steponavičius, deprived of his bishop duties.

Bishop Vincas Sladkevičius, consecrated in 1957, but deprived of his bishop duties.

Vilnius cathedral, now an art gallery.

A concert in Vilnius cathedral.

St. Casimir Church, Vilnius, converted to a Museum of Atheism.

Interior of St. Michael Church, 200 years old,
used as a warehouse.

Jesuit church and monastery at Kaunas, closed and adapted for a warehouse.

Church of the Sisters of St. Casimir, Pažaislis, closed.

The new church at Klaipėda, completed in 1960. The steeple has been torn down and the church is used as a concert hall.

The Mount of the Crosses, near Šiauliai. The communists have destroyed the crosses.

Nukryžiuotojo pietų pertrauka.

"The Crucified Having a Lunch Break"—A typical cartoon mocking religion. Jaunimo Gretos, 1964. No. 9.

"The First Steps." Šluota, August, 1965.

Those who were later granted amnesty and returned to Lithuania are still being harassed at every turn. Their "trans-gressions" are flaunted in the press and at atheist meetings and lectures, and the above-named book is used by propa-gandists as a source of arguments in that ceaseless Com-munist occupation—the "unmasking" of priests.

THE CLERGY IS SILENCED

However malicious the accusations may be, a priest is given no opportunity to defend himself. No newspaper will print a correction of statements made against him or a de-nial of his guilt. In the rare exceptions when it does so, it is only to damage him even more. No court will try a case of libel or slander against a priest. The Soviet Constitu-tion's guarantee of freedom of anti-religious propaganda is interpreted as permitting everyone to speak and write against faith, the church, and the clergy in any way he wishes, but as giving no right to anyone to intercede on behalf of the church or its clergy, nor to a priest to defend himself. This is the "equality" before the law which the Communists have created for their citizens. When one or another priest tried in a sermon to refute the slanderous statements made against him, this conduct was branded as "hooliganism," and he was sentenced to hooligan-type pun-ishment—a fortnight of sweeping streets and cleaning public lavatories.

The clergy may not criticize atheistic propaganda. In the columns of a teachers' journal[34] there appeared a reply to an unpublished letter written by Father Vladas Šlevas to the Vilnius Tiesa. From the reply we learn that Father

---

[34] Tarybinis Mokytojas, February 23, 1960.

Šlevas had suggested introducing the study of religion in school or else withdrawing the course in atheism. The pupils should be allowed to choose between the two subjects. The atheist-teacher who wrote the reply likened religion to refuse and poison, which cannot be compared with atheism. He pointed out at some length that Father Šlevas had gone too far. Following this public denunciation, the priest received an order to transfer to another place.

Another letter to the editor brought its writer, Father Al. Markaitis, more serious consequences. Because he had expressed indignation at a literary journal's[35] disparaging and erroneous treatment of the subject of the Middle Ages, he was not only replied to as a defender of the dark ages, but he subsequently landed in Mordovia, in a forced labor camp.

PROTESTS FROM THE LAITY

Lay persons, too, show their courage by defending their religious beliefs in letters to newspapers. A farmers' semi-weekly, *Valstiečių Laikraštis* (May 26, 1963), published a letter from the Catholic women of a collective farm in the Pasvalys district. It said:

> We should like to ask why they write against God if they say He does not exist? Why is no respect shown to priests? Why do they find fault with parents who bring up their children religiously? It seems to us that without faith in God and in the immortality of the soul, man would resemble a worthless creature, an insignificant little insect. Like others, a believing person is capable of attaining an honorable position in his work. We all work at least 300 to 400 days a year. We win

---

[35] *Literatūra ir Menas,* December 24, 1960.

awards for our work. We feel that religious faith does not impede one's work; on the contrary, it gives life a noble purpose.

A young girl writing in *Tiesa* (December 22, 1960) expressed disagreement with atheistic propaganda:

> My life from my very infancy has been linked with religion, with the Church. Arguments of whatever sort that there is no God will not destroy my faith. As a Catholic, I attend church dutifully and see quite a few priests, but I have never met any of the type described in the newspapers. They exaggerate beyond bounds every mistake of a priest. Of course, among a large number of priests there may be a few such as you write about, but does it mean that they all are like that?
>
> I am only 20 years old. My life is still before me. I find many good points in present-day life. I work and I study. . . . I cannot divide my heart into two parts when it all belongs to the Church. Religion is my very heart, and to take away my religion would be to tear out my heart.

In the same newspaper former priest J. Ragauskas replied to this letter as follows:

> Strange! You are a 20-year-old girl, deeply religious, while I am a 50-year-old man, an atheist. It appears that there is nothing in common between us—youth and old age, religion and atheism, fire and water. Is it really impossible to find a common language?

Ragauskas then explained that he too had been a believer, but had later recognized his error and become a Communist and an atheist. Therefore, the day is coming when the girl, convinced by "scientific evidence," will also stop believing in God. As for priests, whom he knew well, he said, they were all egoists, parasites, and exploiters of the working man.

A PRIEST'S LOT—CONSTANT INTERFERENCE

In light of earlier practice, once a priest was accused in the press of some outrageous crime, one could be almost cer' tain that a scandalous trial was in the offing, after which it would be imprisonment or exile to Siberia. But today the the Communist tactics is to reduce further the clergy's still Knowing that the populace still loves and respects its priests, the Communist tactic is to reduce further the clergy's still substantial authority. This, of course, is not easy. The peo' ple know their priests, their work, and the conditions under which they labor. Sharing the same hardships and depriva' tions, the people place no credence in the Communist charges, but are drawn even closer to the harassed clergy. The cur' rent "corrective" procedure in handling an active priest, after exposing his "offenses" in the press, is to transfer him, on orders from the Commissar for Cult Affairs, to an iso' lated place, often outside his own diocese.

Another way to "straighten out" a priest undesirable to the Communists is to suspend him from all parish duties, allowing him only to say Mass. In extreme cases he may be completely "deregistered" and even his Mass privileges are taken away. Thus completely suspended as a cleric, he is obliged to seek other employment; if unsuccessful, he is sent to Siberia or elsewhere for forced labor duty. The number of such suspended priests is growing larger, and very few of them are reinstated.

Even when transferred, a priest is not permitted to enjoy a peaceful existence. Local Communists, making use of pre' viously published material and "evidence," "enlighten" the people at meetings and various gatherings as to the type of character that has appeared on the scene. A priest's influence is thus impaired from the start. The more zealous priests are not permitted to stay long in one place, but are constantly being transferred for "violations of Soviet laws."

Sometimes in the Communist press one comes on an account of a priest that sounds almost laudatory, until one discovers that the article has an ulterior motive: to bring him to the attention of the authorities. An article which appeared in a teachers' publication[36] is a good example of this type of reporting:

> Not far from Vilnius, in the district of Trakai, on a small elevation, there rises the Church of Rikantai. From afar one hears the tolling of its bells. A stone wall surrounds the church, the burial ground, the orchard, and the pastor's house. Inside this peculiar fortress is Pastor Jonas Kozakas, managing the household.
>
> Every day the respectfully-stooped faithful trudge across the stone barrier. They are mostly persons well along in years who have been attending church for decades. However, among the parishioners you will meet not only grandmothers and grandfathers. Many of the school's eighth-grade pupils also exemplarily attend church. On the terrace of the pastor's residence, children are being prepared for First Communion. They hammer out from memory pages of catechism. . . . In the beginning, the parents lead their children to church, as they say, "by their little hand." Then the pastor subtly and ingeniously gains possession of the young souls and entwines them with a cobweb of "the true faith."
>
> You will ask: Where, then, is the school? Where

---

36 Tarybinis Mokytojas, June 6, 1963.

is the public? Why can't the collective of pedagogues
subdue the priest with their moral force?

These are the very questions that disturb me on
my way to Rikantai. I enter inside the stone enclosure.
I meet a gray-haired, cassocked priest (born 1889), of
pleasing countenance. We are seated in the orchard
on a bench almost submerged in flowers. The priest
smiles pleasantly. I ask him how he manages to get so
many people to church.

—"The believers come by themselves. I do not
entice them."

—"Don't you find anti-religious propaganda, lectures, talks interfering?"

—"They don't interfere." The priest again smiles
pleasantly. "When there is an anti-religious concert
or meeting at the school or club, I change the time of
the masses. From their gathering they go directly to
church. . . ."

Then the correspondent, who was a government agent,
described his visit with the school director, from whom he
learned that anti-religious work in that area was being ne-
glected, that the club was offering no opposition to the
pastor's school, and that the club's woman director, upon
leaving the club, began openly to attend church. All were
indifferent to atheistic work.

Well, Pastor Kozakas has good reason to smile
pleasantly. As in earlier days, dozens of pupils from the
first to the eighth grade kiss his wrinkled hand. "Re-
placements are coming up." Jonas Kozakas pleasantly
pats the tousled little heads.

Conclusion: Soon afterward Pastor Kozakas of Rikantai
was dislodged from his "fortress" and transferred to a place
which had no school.

Such are the working conditions of Lithuania's priests.

XI. SOVIET ATTITUDE TOWARD OTHER RELIGIONS

BEFORE WORLD WAR II, Lithuania's Protestants numbered about 240,000, with the Klaipėda area accounting for 153,-000. The four Klaipėda districts had 64 Protestant churches. Scattered through the rest of the country were 52 Lutheran parishes and 12 parishes of the Protestant Reformed Church. As provided by the Constitution, state support of Protestant churches in 1939 amounted to 114,360 litas.

When Hitler annexed Klaipėda in 1939, Lithuania's Protestant population was substantially reduced. Even the larger, unannexed part of the country lost 40,000 Protestants, who as "Volksdeutsche" (their German nationality being determined by their Protestant faith) and in accordance with the secret agreement between Ribbentrop and Molotov on August 23, 1939, were transferred to Germany. Among those moved out of Lithuania were 22 Lutheran pastors, five Reformed Church pastors and superintendents of both denominations.

WHEN THE COMMUNISTS MOVED IN

When the Soviets occupied Lithuania in 1940, no distinctions were made among the various religions—all were purveyors of "religious superstition." Together with Catholics, Protestants suffered the same deprivations and persecution: their press was closed, their financial assets were confiscated, their churches and other property were expropriated by the Bolsheviks for their own needs. For example, the lovely Lutheran church in Vilnius was made into a Communist Youth headquarters. From the historical Lutheran church at Kėdainiai, its artistically-made pews and Founders' Throne were sawed up and thrown out, and the church itself was converted into a granary. The Lutheran church in Kaunas became a bridge sentry post, and the Marijampolė church a dance-hall.

When the Klaipėda area fell into Russian hands during the second Soviet occupation, of the 153,000 Protestants residing there, 47,740 fled to West Germany, about 45,000 moved to East Germany, about 20,000 became ware casualties, and about 41,000 remained behind in Klaipėda.

In the course of military action, many of the churches in Klaipėda, such as St. John's and St. Jacob's, and others in the outlying areas, were destroyed. Those left standing were taken over by the Soviets. For instance, the church at Palaičiai was used as a stable and later made into a storage depot. Similar fate befell the Protestant churches elsewhere in Lithuania: the Garliava Church is now used for grain storage; the church at Šiauliai is a museum. Likewise, at Kėdainiai, Skirsnemunė, and Žiemelis, the churches were expropriated for purposes far removed from the worship of God. One, at Jurbarkas, was even used for a jail.

Following their penchant for desecrating and destroying church burial grounds, the Communists installed swings and dancing facilities in the cemetery at Vitėnai, a suburb of Klaipėda, and the chapel was turned into living quarters for Soviet troops. Other cemeteries—Margiai, Grabstai, Šilutė, Panevėžys—were made into athletic fields.

LIVING WITH ENDLESS HARASSMENT

When the Soviets occupied Lithuania the second time, only ten Protestant ministers were left in the entire country. Since these few could not possibly provide adequate service to the Protestant community, the faithful were forced to rely on their own selected lay preachers to lead them in worship with hymns, prayer, and the Word of God. An especially strong manifestation of this form of religious service was prevalent among the Protestants in the Klaipėda area. During the Soviet occupation, some of these lay preachers assumed full pastoral duties. In Klaipėda, where no church was available to the Lutherans, the service was conducted by preacher Bläsner in private homes. Since the Communist authorities forbid these new clergymen from performing religious rites, Protestant worship goes on in secret, and the lay preachers spend their days performing full-time duties on collective farms or other Soviet-controlled enterprise.

During the Stalin era, Protestant clergymen in Lithuania were permitted to teach catechism to the children and to prepare them for Confirmation. Since then, however, these privileges have been abrogated, and any attempt "to spread superstition and inflict harm on the child's conscience," as in the case of Catholics, is punishable by law.

The Protestant clergyman, too, is subject to moral terrorism. He is driven to making public confessions and renunciations of his faith. One recent victim of such terror was the 80-year-old minister of the Reformed Church, Adomas Šernas, whose article renouncing his faith and clerical duties was printed in *Tiesa* on August 16, 1964, a few months before he died.

Small religious communities of Baptists, Biblists, Adventists, and Jehovah's Witnesses—all comparatively new to the Lithuanian scene and operating secretly—are a special object of Communist attention. The very membership in these denominations, which are not registered with the govern- ment, is considered a state crime. Their preachers are said to declare in strong terms that the Communist system is the work of the devil and must be avoided: one may not obey its orders, serve in its army, or send one's children to a Com- munist school. This type of doctrine finds considerable appeal among those who have lost faith in the Communist cause. The authorities find it difficult to put an end to these reli- gious groups, for new adherents are constantly arriving from Russia. On March 19, 1961, the newspaper *Komjaunimo Tiesa* warned the Communist authorities that the hostility of these Christian religions toward Communist ideology is turning into outright disloyalty to the Soviet system.

Most of the followers of these denominations are con- centrated in Vilnius and are especially strong in factories and among railroad workers. They are not numerous among Lithuanians, at least in Lithuania, but one comes across Lith- uanian names more frequently of late among preachers being searched for or receiving long prison sentences in Siberia.

Government security organs investigated the doings of the Jehovah's Witnesses. The findings were disclosed in the Russian humorous and satirical publication *Krokodil* in 1961: The Witnesses are active in forced labor camps and hold their meetings at night. Their motto is: "Be still as a dove and poisonous as a snake." The chief culprit is Jonas Bar- kauskas, who persuaded a woman and her son to join the Witnesses; preaching the Commandment "Thou shalt not kill," he dissuades young men from serving in the army. The Witnesses receive pamphlets from Brooklyn: "Watchtower," "The Service of Heaven," "My Dear Brother," which they reproduce and circulate. Leader of another secret group is Kazlauskas, formerly an associate of an American spy identified as "Williams." All this takes place in Mine No. 18, Konjakovka, Chernyakhovsk Region, District of Irkutsk.

In Lithuania, February, 1962, the Klaipėda court sentenced the leader of the Witnesses to five years in prison and other members to shorter terms.

In a Vilnius radio broadcast on February 22, 1962, the Jehovah's Witnesses were called "bandits, traitors, participants in anti-Soviet activity, and serpents in the guise of doves." The broadcast stated that this sect first appeared in Lithuania in 1959 and was propagated by a former "bandit." His followers were persons who had already been punished by 10 to 25 years' loss of freedom "for betraying their country and killing Soviet people." Although the Soviet government had permitted them to start a new, decent life, they joined a sect which is harmful to their mind and body.[1]

That same year, the Telšiai court, after a two-day trial, sentenced Irena Micpovilaitis to four years in prison. A graduate of a school of medicine, she was working in the medical section of Mastys factory, where she organized an illegal sect and induced a worker, a nurse, and a patient to join. She also provided her followers with religious literature. Since no one, not even Party and youth organization chiefs, factory heads, or even her sister, was able to persuade her to mend her erring ways, she was convicted for having inflicted "crippling injury on the youth."[2]

---

[1] *Eltos Informacijos,* March 3, 1962.
[2] *Komjaunimo Tiesa,* March 19, 1961.

If members of any of these religious denominations are found to be "mutilating" their children, they, like the Catholics, are deprived by court action of their parental rights, and the children are placed in the custody of state institutions.

XII. RESISTANCE BY THE FAITHFUL

IT IS COMFORTING to find the Christian way of life still flourishing—quietly, perhaps, but surely—amid all the obstacles.
Of this we learn from the Communists themselves.

In the May 30, 1963, issue of *Tiesa*, S. Markonis accused the intellectuals that they still view life through a
religious prism. He rebuked the teachers who come to class
on religious feast-days dressed in their Sunday best and who
assume a fine manner, thereby unwittingly emphasizing the
day's significance. Even worse, some teachers attend church
and observe religious customs at home. Others intentionally
avoid discussing atheistic topics, purposely cast disparaging
remarks about contentious atheists, and associate themselves
with believers more eagerly than with atheists. Complaint
is made that some teachers are atheists in school, "but when
they land in another district, betake themselves to church
to pray."

In the first four grades of the Joniškis district schools, a
large percentage of the pupils answering a questionnaire
admitted their belief in God. Another large portion of the
pupils replied ambiguously. Whether there were any outright non-believers, the newspaper reporting this did not say.[1]

In one of the schools, a visiting inspector from the Department of Education found a handsome showcase display
denying the existence of God. The inspector was sure that

---

[1] *Tarybinis Mokytojas,* June 9, 1963.

117

all the children there were good little atheists. Standing beside this display, he asked the pupils, "Where does God
live?" To his amazement, came the reply, "In heaven, in
church, and everywhere."[2]

Expressive of the Christian attitude that still prevails in
the hearts and the minds of some of Lithuania's inhabitants
are these excerpts from a letter that found its way to the
West:

> Periodicals are full of discussions and searching for
> ways to draw people away from the church. Old pagan
> customs are being propagated, merely so that "the bells
> not toll." How must the faithful feel amidst this torrent
> of propaganda? What must the clergy feel?
>
> Today, as I was making my Way of the Cross, the
> Eleventh Station brought to my mind an analagous sit-
> uation: You, Christ, were disrobed and humiliated be-
> fore the crowd. Today our priests and the faithful are
> undergoing similar treatment. You were taunted with
> the cry, "If you are God, step down from the cross.
> Help yourself." Today they cry out to us, "Where
> is your God? Why does He not protect you? Why
> does He not stay the godless?"
>
> The early Christians died heroically for Christ. How
> many today would give up their life for their faith?
> But this is not even required. Today a believing person
> must dwindle away, suffocate, decay—an unknown,
> repudiated being, converted almost to an idiot. That
> is the greatest tragedy. It is reducing a living being to
> a mummy.
>
> There is one consolation—that God sees all; that
> the gates of hell shall not prevail against the Church;
> that heaven and earth shall pass away, but His words
> shall not pass away. And finally, "when therefore you
> shall see the abomination of desolation, which was

---

[2] *Lietuvių Religinė Informacija*, July 30, 1963.

spoken of by Daniel the prophet, standing in the holy place, know that the time is near." That "abomination of desolation" we already see: in place of the altar there is a stage; where there was kneeling there is dancing; where there was praying there is blasphemy.

I have nothing against atheism that desires and seeks the truth. Such atheism will one day end at the feet of God. But I hate slanderous and blasphemous atheism, especially when the slandered are given no chance to reply, to defend themselves.

ATHEIST DOCTRINE ALIEN, UNCONVINCING

Faith is not a garment, which can be torn off at will. This has been proved in the Soviet Union itself, which for nearly 50 years has carried on anti-religious propaganda, accompanied by terrorization, the closing of Russian Orthodox churches, the killing of its clergy by the thousands, and mass deportations of the faithful. Yet during the war, when Stalin allowed the church a bit more freedom, in an effort to rally his people to make a stand against the Germans, about 50,000,000 inhabitants were soon enrolled in parishes, and the rest, though not officially members of the church, had God in their hearts. After years of "scientific" education, and with the younger generation brought up without any understanding of God and even predisposed against all religion, the government finds it necessary to cry out that "religious archaisms" are still strong and that surer means must be found to destroy them.

It is even more difficult to destroy religious faith in Lithuania, where the nation has clung to it for centuries as to an irreplaceable value. Although many of Lithuania's churches are today closed, the hierarchy almost wiped out, and the number of priests reduced, religious belief has not been rooted out of the people's hearts. Many anti-religious lecturers about whom the press writes are not volunteers, but have been forcibly pressed into service. The audiences that come to hear them are there not of their own choice. Knowing that true atheists were a rarity in independent Lithuania and that atheism had no success among the people, it is difficult to believe that the present-day godless are the atheists they profess to be. It is only the current environment which has brought them into being. This explains the lack of enthusiasm and fervor for which Party leaders constantly reproach them. Even if all of the 70,000 persons belonging to the Communist Party were atheist, that would still come to only 2.3 per cent of the population. If all the youth be-longing to the *Komsomol*—officially there were 200,000 members in 1963—were atheist, we would have to view the situation with anxiety. But it is no secret, even to the Com-munists, that quite a few *Komsomol* and Party members publicly avail themselves of the religious rites of the church and even a larger number do so secretly. Many of those held to be genuine Communists and good atheists conceal their religious practice by attending church far from their place of residence.

EVIDENCE OF RELIGIOUS FERVOR

One indication of the people's devotion to their faith is the number of persons receiving the sacraments. For example, in the Archdiocese of Kaunas, 21,000 received the sacra-ment of Confirmation in 1959 alone. During an octave at Šiluva, when help from the neighboring clergy was still per-mitted, 30,000 Communions used to be distributed. In Vil-nius, in 1960, at St. Teresa's Church and its Chapel of *Aušros Vartai* (Our Lady of Vilnius), 150,000 received

Holy Communion, about 1,000 were baptized, and 100,000 Confessions were heard. At St. Michael's Church, the same year, there were 70,000 communicants. On two feast-days at the Way of the Cross Church in Vilnius, 120,000 Communions were distributed.

CHURCH ATTENDANCE

It is true that church attendance is not as high as it was in 1940-41 (during the first Soviet occupation), but it is far higher than the Communists claim. Many go to church, perform their religious duties secretly, and are never included in Communist-gathered statistics. Living under a system of spying, intrigue, provocation, and accusation, people have learned to hide their convictions, to conceal their religious practice, and to be silent on the subject of religion. Otherwise they are terrorized and compelled to declare themselves publicly as non-believers. It is, therefore, not surprising that occasional tourists and journalists from abroad do not get a true picture of the religious situation. Some, observing that the churches are well-attended on holy days, conclude that the country is still deeply religious; others, after a chat with tourist guides, are convinced that religion is all but eradicated.

One who recently came to the West related how, on a random visit to a church in Alytus, he met a doctor, a teacher, and a student—all from different localities.

Another person now living in the West recalls his own conduct thus:

Not wanting to hurt others, I shall talk only about myself. For several years I expounded to *Komsomol* groups at Raseiniai the "indestructible" principles of

materialism. But whenever I visited Kaunas, I would
stop off at a church and go to confession. Several times
I was sent to Kaunas to attend a course in Materialism-
Marxism-Atheism, and after I had had my fill of the
wisdom of "the sages," on the way back I would pay
a visit to the Shrine of Our Lady of Šiluva and there
unburden myself of my sorrows.

A primary school teacher in one of the larger cities wrote
to her friend in the West:

> I went to Vilnius, where I hadn't been for several
> years. I stayed there several days and spent nearly all
> of my time at the well-known Gate.[3] I had a good cry
> and eased my heart.

RELIGIOUS RITUALS WIDELY OBSERVED

As far as is known, there are very few unbaptized children in Lithuania. The Vilnius radio on May 29, 1961,
remarked:

> It is truly strange that often even atheists permit
> their children to be baptized in church. They yield to
> the influence of pious women and humble themselves
> before superstition. Every servile act is shameful; it
> helps to retain the remnants of superstition. It makes
> people think that atheists only pretend to be such,
> while actually they reason differently if they baptize
> their children.

The dead are rarely buried without religious services.
Even in "Communist" burials, the family in most cases
makes use of a priest's services, including a secret blessing of

---

[3] The reference is to the shrine, the Gate of Dawn, object of pilgrimages,
containing the miraculous painting of Our Lady of Vilnius.

the grave and, earlier, ministration of the sacraments to the dying. So unpopular is burial without a priest that, para' doxically, some priests have been punished for refusing to bury prominent Communists in sanctified ground and with a church service when the deceased had not made his peace with the Church.

The same attitude prevails with respect to church mar' riages. Very few content themselves with only a civil marriage ceremony and the gift that goes with it; usually they follow this with a religious marriage, either in their own church or farther away from home. The Communists are particularly incensed that this is being practiced by Party members and by their own select youth of the *Komsomol.* But obviously such deviations from proper Party procedure is quite common, and the Communists are resigned to it.

The attachment to religious practices which persists in Lithuania is revealed by a young woman's reply to Party members who had attacked her for having a church wedding. She replied, as reported in a Communist Youth newspaper,[4] "I knew that my husband's parents were religious, so I agreed to a church marriage. I didn't want to make things unpleasant for them. Besides, my husband, too, wanted a church marriage." Reminded that both were members of the *Komsomol,* she replied, "Yes, but we wanted a serious marriage. What's wrong with that?"

In another instance, when it was discovered that a Party member had been married in church, the secretary of the Party organization of Jūra collective farm addressed him in the journal *Komunistas* (May, 1961) as follows: "By having a church marriage you withdrew from a position of mate' rialist viewpoint and yielded to the whims of your wife. In

---

4 *Komjaunimo Tiesa,* August 3, 1963.

whose name have you done so?" There was, of course, no reply.

A veterinary assistant in Šiauliai was reprimanded in the press by the district Communist Youth committee for "bolstering his civil marriage with a church service," and his act was duly noted on his personal record card. His behavior was unworthy of a *Komsomol* atheist, said other press comments. He was permitted, however, to retain his *Komsomol* membership.

To avoid public denunciation, most church marriages take place in secret, and many who are thought to have had only a civil marriage have actually had a church blessing also.

RELIGION AMONG THE YOUTH

One sees manifestations of religious feeling among youngsters in school, who are a special target of atheistic propaganda. They are not always easy to hold in line. Many of them hide their beliefs. Some are also courageous and dare to profess their faith openly.

One high school student, who ranked first in his class, was given for his final examination a written assignment on an atheistic topic. The young man wrote his composition, but as he handed it to the teacher, he disavowed what he had written, for he believed in God. Then, with tears in his eyes, he walked out of the class.

A rather worrisome reference was made at a conference on atheism that "some Lithuanian students, on completing their examinations, thank God!"[5]

Prof. J. Kauneckas admitted[6] that there were still many religious students, and he urged everyone to work closely

---

[5] See "Ateistinė Propaganda Lietuvoje," *Draugas*, August 4, 1962.
[6] *Tiesa*, October 7, 1961.

with them and, by using scientific proof, to convince them of "religion's absurdity."

Another university professor complained that on holy days one may see many students in church "demonstratively" showing off their student caps.

In 1962, the University of Vilnius had a widely-discussed trial, conducted by the History and Philology Department. A student was charged with not only being openly religious, but also with having tried to induce others to a similar line of belief. In the presence of students and professors, all tried to convince him of the error of his ways, but the accused zealously defended his viewpoint and, in his final statement, stressed his belief in God. The university court decided that such a "backward" person could no longer attend the university. It is noteworthy that his student colleagues sided with him and tried to defend him.

At times youth hits upon ingenious ways of defying atheistic terror. For example, in Lithuania's capital city of Vilnius, just as the Communists were congratulating themselves on having dealt a death blow to religion, the young people of the city, virtually en masse, began wearing little crosses on their breast. The Communists were quick to explain[7] that the sudden outbreak of cross-wearing had no religious significance and had occurred only because, "in a Paris fashion magazine, a cross was shown as the newest note in costume accessories."

Speaking of crosses, it might be mentioned that Lithuania's roadsides, farm settlements, and cemeteries were for a long time dotted with artistic, hand-crafted crosses, for which Lithuania earned the title "Land of the Crosses." The Communists, averse to religious symbols, have destroyed over

[7] *Komjaunimo Tiesa*, August 3, 1963.

8,000 of these crosses and hundreds of other folk shrines. There were instances when some courageous souls would set up new crosses in their place, but these too would be torn down or burnt. More recently, it was reported[8] that "a pilgrim" named Ringys succeeded in erecting a stone cross at night. Worst of all, he was helped by young farm workers who officially claim to be non-believers.

At a conference of atheist propagandists, the director of the Vilnius Museum of Atheism sought to find out why young doctors on finishing their medical training still believed in "religious superstitions."

PROPAGANDISTS' WORK MADE DIFFICULT

The people use every possible excuse to avoid attending the lectures and discussions that the Communists organize across the country. When forced to attend, they stare listlessly or doze. The fact that women show little interest in atheist lectures was explained by the editor of a woman's magazine, *Tarybinė Moteris* (November, 1961): After putting in a whole day at their domestic duties, the women were just too tired to concentrate on atheistic "enlightenment"; their minds were more on their homes and children.

A report in the same publication informs us that the woman who dominated an atheist conference at Seirijai in 1961 was the author of a magazine article titled "Why I Don't Believe." However, Marija Severenskas, sculptress, who was to speak on how she had freed herself of "religious superstitions," was unable to be present; her husband had forbidden her to attend. The article remarked on the passivity of the audience: "You see a person sitting, seemingly listen-

---

8 *Tiesa,* September 27, 1963.

ing, but not a muscle in his face shows the slightest quiver.
It is as though a gray, colorless mask had covered his features. One wishes to pass a hand across such face and thus,
perhaps, wipe off that expression of indifference."

A lecturer at a collective farm in the District of Mažeikiai asked an elderly woman just returned from church what
the priest had said in his sermon. The woman replied: "Collective farm goods are common property. Therefore, we may
appropriate a part of these goods and God will not punish
us for it."

At another gathering, this same propagator of atheism
was challenged as to the accuracy of his references to a
prominent clergyman. After being called a liar to his face,
he concluded that it is better to involve the listeners in
arguments among themselves rather than with the lecturer.
He also advised his fellow lecturers to use folk humor.[9]

Propagandists are urged to be clever in their work. Were
it not for his own shrewdness, a lecturer proudly boasted, a
collective farm workers' meeting in the District of Šakiai
would not have heard his atheistic lecture about Easter. But
when he saw that the audience was beginning to disperse
as soon as the general meeting was over and without waiting
for the lecture, he was clever enough to pose the question,
"Don't you want to hear about the Pope's recent letters to
the Christians?" The audience was thus intrigued and stayed
to listen to his planned lecture.[10]

It is the workers on collective farms who are the propagandists' most baffling problem. First, because of the living
conditions, the workers would welcome dismissal from their
work. Second, there is a feeling of solidarity among them.

[9] *Tiesa,* August 31, 1961.
[10] *Komunistas,* April, 1961.

They act collectively: they themselves decide which holidays to observe, they use communal vehicles for transportation to church, etc. When forced to attend lectures, they boldly argue with the speaker and later send him unpleasant, anony- mous letters. A writer admitted in a Vilnius radio broadcast that he himself had received such letters, one of which said, "Young man, it is not too late to make peace with God. Consider what you're doing."[11]

In another broadcast on January 14, 1963, a Commu- nist official attacked Party organizations for allowing col- lective farm workers to observe holy days (referring to Christmas). Their absence from work for several days, he said, affects the Soviet farm output. He castigated the local Communists for sitting on their hands and not persuading these religious addicts that work was far more important than holy days and "religious superstitions."

Chairmen of collective farms are constantly reminded that they are far too accommodating to "the churchmen." *Raudonoji Žvaigždė* (The Red Star) was indignant that a pastor had been given a plot of ground three times as large as that received by other workers and permitted to use the farm horses to bring home hay and firewood. Even worse, the young people were allowed to use the farm truck to take them to church on Sundays and holy days. "It often happens that one can hear religious music and choir songs emanating from a packed church, while the Culture House, which ought to be the center of atheist activity, remains closed at that time."[12]

The Propaganda Section of the Communist Party Central Committee has been exploring the reasons why propaganda

---

[11] *Eltos Informacijos,* October 27, 1962.
[12] *Lietuvių Religinė Informacija,* January 26, 1963.

and "scientific enlightenment" do not seem to help, and why the people remain religious. Of special interest is the religiosity of the workers on collective farms; these persons were to be offered individual instruction. An investigation in the Kėdainiai district revealed a great diversity among the believers "in the level of their belief and in their viewpoint. Some based their attitude toward the Church on their belief in supernatural powers, others on the authority of the clergy, identification of religion with morality, the strength of religious traditions, etc.[13]

On tours of "investigation and instruction" of collective farms, the propagandists hear from ordinary workers that a non-believer cannot be a decent person; that when one condemns the clergy, one need not by the same act condemn religion. In the district of Vilkaviškis they heard one man state flatly: "We are all Catholics, and we want our children to be the same." From their collected evidence, the propagandists have concluded that religious belief is a means of expressing dissatisfaction with the present order existing in Lithuania.[14]

When a magazine reviled two sisters for organizing a church choir and participating in other parish activity, a Vilnius University student, Adolfas Jatulis, protested in a letter to the editor:[15]

Why are these girls being attacked? Is it only be-cause they believe in God? But that is unjust. . . . You claim that the Lazdenis sisters haven't done a good thing in all their lives. But I know that they were always conscientious in their work on the collective farm. One

---

[13] *Komunistas,* September, 1961.
[14] *Komunistas,* November, 1962.
[15] *Literatūra ir Menas,* December 24, 1960.

of them even had her photo placed on the Honor Board as one of the best workers in the area. . . . It is our duty to fight for human rights. It seems to me that it is unjust to publish false accusations.

The student acknowledged at the end that he was so upset by this grave injustice that he was unable to write further. This elicited the editor's attack on Jatulis:

The musty fumes of melting wax and burning incense emanating from the churches have evidently dulled your senses and befogged your eyes, so that you are unable to see reality. . . . Haven't you drawn nearer to Lithuanian bourgeois nationalists on the other side of the Atlantic? They too would like to write off our advances. So that is the camp toward which your defense of religious philosophy is pulling you.

Then, an outright threat:

It is impossible to stay silent when a Soviet student conducts himself this way. It is something that Jatulis' classmates and their Communist Youth organizations, whose duty it is to educate those who, with diploma in hand, will be going out to teach the younger generation, ought well to ponder.

After this, Jatulis was dismissed from the university, for to defend religion and the faithful against unwarranted attack is an offense against Communist "truth."

Religion continues to have its propagators, who pursue their objective undaunted by Communist denunciations and threats in the press. The Communist *Tiesa* itself, on September 28, 1963, published a news report of a young girl at a *Komsomol* meeting at *Taika* (Peace) collective farm in the

Kaunas District, who was caught reading a religious book while the meeting was in progress. Questioned, she admitted that she had received the book from a certain Paulius Petronis, medical worker. Further investigation revealed that this Petronis, under the pretext of teaching folksongs to a group of women at the Culture House, was actually teaching religious songs, and this not only to women, but to young Communists as well. He was working under the banner of the Temperance Society.

At a meeting of propaganda specialists, the Lithuanian Academy of Sciences was accused of failing to exploit the achievements of the cosmonauts for the atheist cause. At the same time, atheists were urged to give more attention to the subject of morality, since atheism is blamed by clergymen for drunkenness, disruption of families, and all other vices.[16]

GOD REMAINS A PROBLEM

The influence of the Church remains an object of serious concern to the Communists. In the monthly *Komunistas* (April, 1962) Lithuania's top Communist, Party Secretary Antanas Sniečkus, although agreeing that religion may be a mere habit to many, could not refrain from pointing the finger of accusation at the Church, and reminded his brother atheists that the Church now operates in a more subtle manner, and continually seeks new ways to strengthen its contact with the people, especially the youth. He urged a more effective Communist method of youth training and stressed the use of the press and radio in particular. He added that the Communists must delve more deeply into

---

16 *Komunistas*, April, 1962.

the reasons why the people still cling tenaciously to "religious superstitions."

The people's faith seems to remain unshaken, even despite the new argument that the Soviet cosmonauts had traversed the entire universe and had found no trace of God or heaven. No less an atheist than the then Soviet premier, Nikita S. Khrushchev, in an interview with the *New York Times* cor' respondent, C. L. Sulzberger, on November 5, 1961, elabo' rated on this very theme, relating that, first, Cosmonaut Titov and, later, Cosmonaut Gagarin reported on their return to the earth that there was absolutely nothing that looked like para' dise out in those far reaches of space.

Yet even this, which might be called "the last word" in scientific argument, is recognized by the intellectual and the student as mere sham—a perversion of truth. A think' ing person cannot accept the Communist explanation of the origin and meaning of religion and Christianity. Constantly pounded by blasts of demagoguery, he is stirred to an even greater interest in the entire aspect of religion, and prefers to draw his own conclusions.

AN OMEN OF VICTORY?

Engaged in a gigantic struggle for their most precious human rights and conscious of the indifference of the West' ern World to the persecutions they undergo, the Lithuanian faithful can only pray and hope for divine rescue from their plight. Their faith has been strengthened by what has been described by many as a miraculous apparition, which occurred in July, 1962.

It seems that in the parish of Skiemonys, in the Diocese of Panevėžys, in a field which is part of Janonis collective farm, the Blessed Virgin revealed herself to a young girl,

Roma-Pranciška Macvys and, weeping, complained that there were many godless people in Lithuania. The Virgin urged prayer and fasting on Fridays, and promised to save the world if the people returned to God. The vision was said to have been witnessed by a large group of people.

The incident might have retained its local character, were it not for the wide publicity given to it by *Tiesa* on July 31, 1962. Of course the correspondent mocked the entire affair and accused the pastor of directing the whole spectacle. This was enough to bring out even greater crowds to the site of the vision. Pilgrims came from as far as Latvia, Byelorussia, and the Ukraine. The directors of the collective farm erected a platform on the site, while the people set up an altar and decorated it with candles and flowers.

Though the question of the vision's authenticity must be left to Church authorities, the fact remains that whatever happened at Skiemonys has caused serious concern to the Communists. At first they tried to convince visitors that the vision was only the product of a hallucination. When the propagandists were driven away by crowds of believers, the authorities ordered the platform and the altar to be levelled to the ground with tractors and forbade all further visits to the hallowed spot.

But the people keep coming. Miraculous cures have been reported. The greatest miracle, however, is the return of many atheists to God.

A visitor to this site in July, 1963, the first anniversary of the vision, was deeply impressed:

> I experienced an unforgettable moment, for everything here is very moving. A Communist festival was to have taken place here, but instead the followers of little Roma (the girl before whom the vision appeared)

took over. There is a great multitude here. The roads are jammed with riders and pedestrians, despite the ban on such visits. And I can't tell you the quantities of flowers. . . .

Letters reaching the West express the hope that some day a church may be erected on the site of the reported vision. Though persecuted and "scientifically" indoctrinated by the atheistic occupants of their ancient land, the people are quick and eager, as of old, to seek solace in Mary.